Orangeville Ontario on Broadway in Colour Photos, Saving Our History One Photo at a Time

Photography
by Barbara Raué
2013

Series Name:
Cruising Ontario

Book 51: Orangeville on Broadway

Cover photo: Orangeville Town Hall, 87 Broadway

Series Name: Cruising Ontario

Now in colour
Appendix with Architectural Terms and Building Styles at the
back of each book

Other Books by Barbara Raue

Coins of Gold

Arrows, Indians and Love

The Life and Times of Barbara
Volume 1: Inventions That Have Enhanced My Life
Volume 2: Entertainment That I Have Enjoyed
Volume 3: East Coast Trips
Volume 4: Olympics
Volume 5: Wonders of the World
Volume 6: Caribbean Cruises
Volume 7: Animals
Volume 8: Storms
Volume 9: Wars

The Cromwell Family Book

Visit Barbara's website to view all of her books
http://barbararaue.ericraue.com

Orangeville

John Corbit acquired land in the area in 1829 and is one of the earliest settlers. Spring Brook, a tributary of the Credit River, provided water for power for several mills located downstream.

In 1833 Seneca Ketchum bought 200 acres on the north side of what became Broadway, followed four years later by George Grigg who bought 100 acres on the south side. By 1844 when Orange Lawrence and his wife, Sarah, arrived from Connecticut, a well-established community called Grigg's Mill existed beside Mill Creek. (Mill Creek and Spring Brook were the same tributary of the Credit River.)

Orange Lawrence helped to develop the community. He bought 300 acres, laid out the southeast part of town, bought Grigg's Mill, opened a general store and a tavern, built a second mill, founded the first school, and became the village's first postmaster in 1847. He left a strong mark on the community which took the appropriate name of Orangeville.

Immigrants from Ireland and other parts of the British Isles and Canada West came throughout the 1840s and 1850s with some establishing successful mixed farms while others settled in the village and became the landowners, merchants, and tradesmen whose needs led to the development of good transportation routes.

By the 1860s it was increasingly difficult to deliver and receive goods to and from the supply centres in the south. Mono Road, Centre Road, Trafalgar Road, and the Toronto to Owen Sound Road were gravel roads that were difficult to traverse by horse and wagon for much of the year. Winter was the season when most goods were transported by sleigh over frozen roads.

By 1871 two daily stage lines were operating between Orangeville and Brampton, and that year the Toronto, Grey and Bruce Railway, a narrow gauge rail line, reached Orangeville, thanks to the efforts of town fathers such as Jesse Ketchum Jr., Samuel and Robert McKitrick, Johnston Lindsey, Thomas Jull, John Foley, and Dr. William Armstrong.

By 1875 there was a foundry, three planing mills, two saw mills, a tannery, a carding mill, several carriage and wagon manufacturers, and a successful pottery business in operation, along with four grocers, three hardware merchants, two drugstores, three watchmakers, three bakeries, and three establishments providing boots and shoes.

It was the foresight of Orange Lawrence and Jesse Ketchum that had large sections of land on either side of the main street laid out for both commercial and residential building lots. The south side followed Mill Creek while a regular grid pattern was determined for the streets on the north side from First to Fifth Streets both east and west and north to Fifth Avenue, with a wide main street called Broadway. This 30-metre (100-foot) avenue was not typical of Ontario towns of the time, but has proven to be very valuable over the years. In 1875 the Town Hall was constructed, and in 1887 the first telephone exchange was established, and in 1916 electricity came to the town.

The old town of Orangeville is still alive today. Some of the buildings on Broadway have been demolished; others have been renovated, while others remain as they were when they were built 120 years ago.

There are hundreds of old buildings in Orangeville which have retained their 1800s architectural styles and character. The first Orangeville book covers the beginnings of Orangeville with pictures from the south side of town. An appendix is included to describe architectural styles and terms which are referred to throughout the book. The second book covers buildings on Broadway.

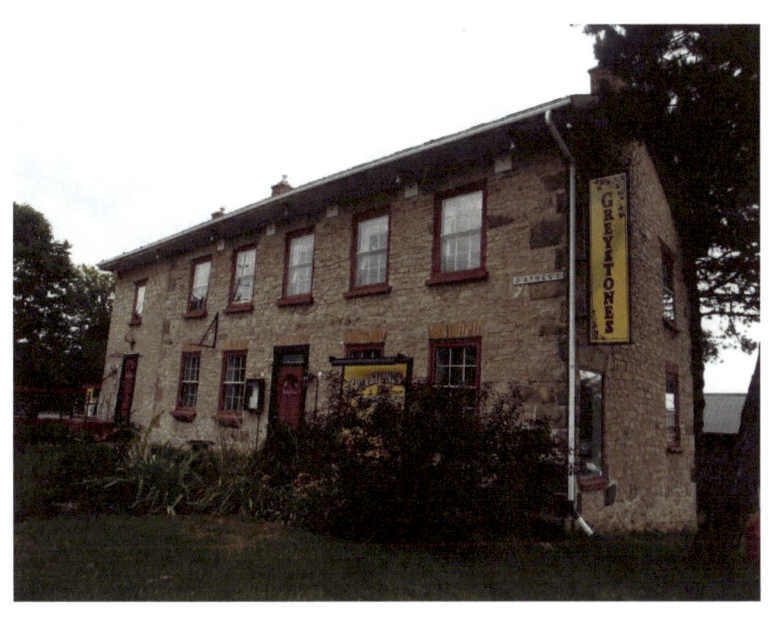

63 Broadway – James Graham – Tavern Keeper c. 1852
Greystones Inn – Georgian style

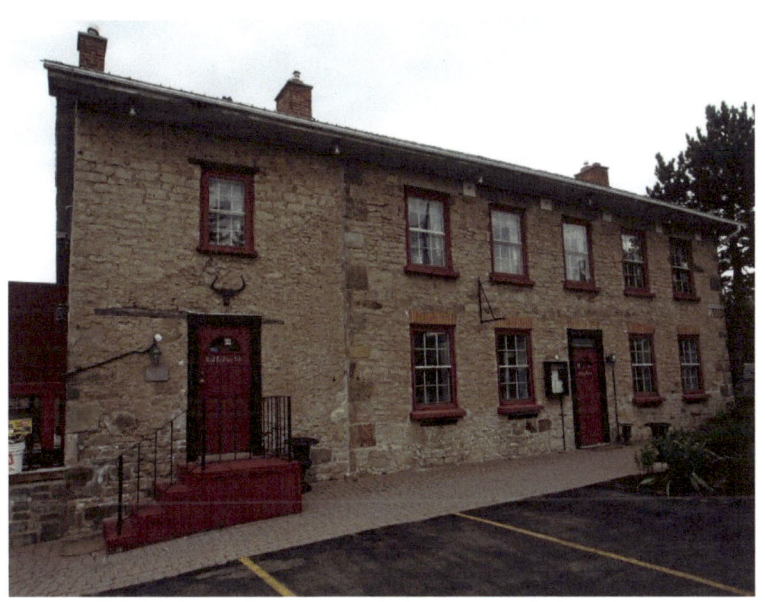

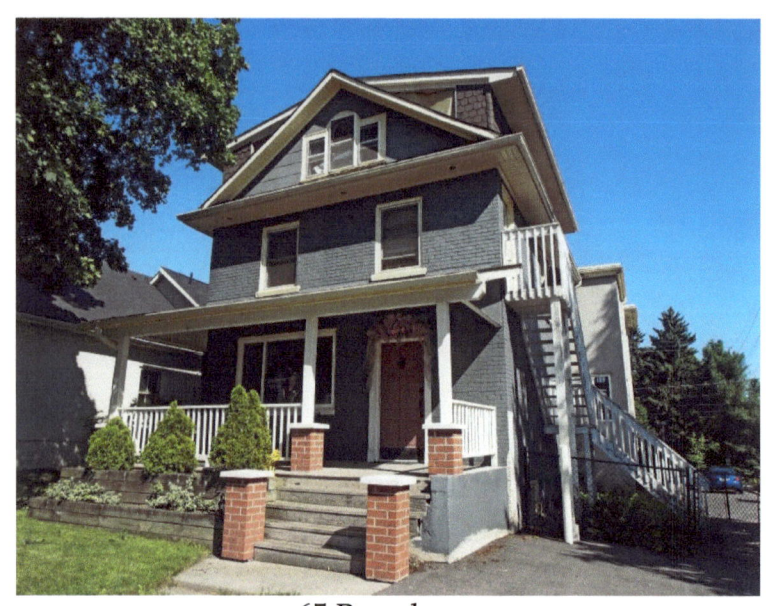

65 Broadway
Edwardian Classicism – large triangular front gable with
Palladian window and shallow roofed porch

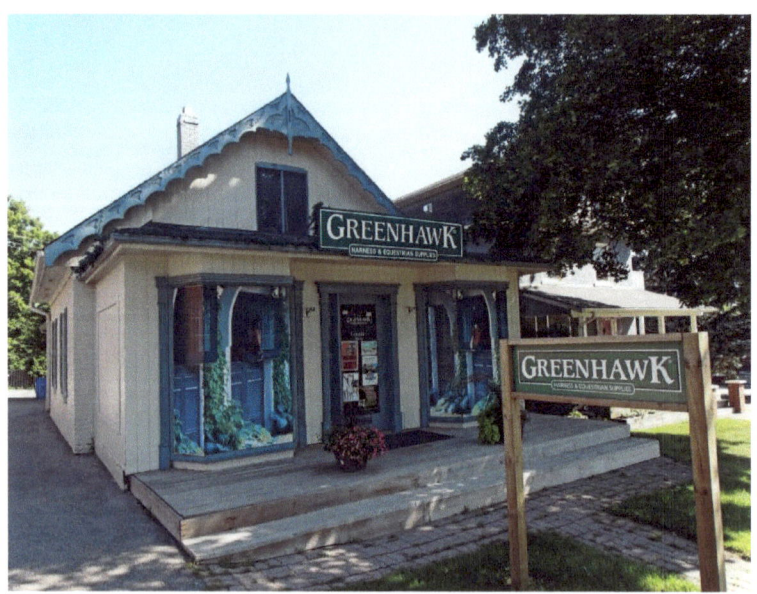

Gothic Revival style – Vergeboard trim on gable

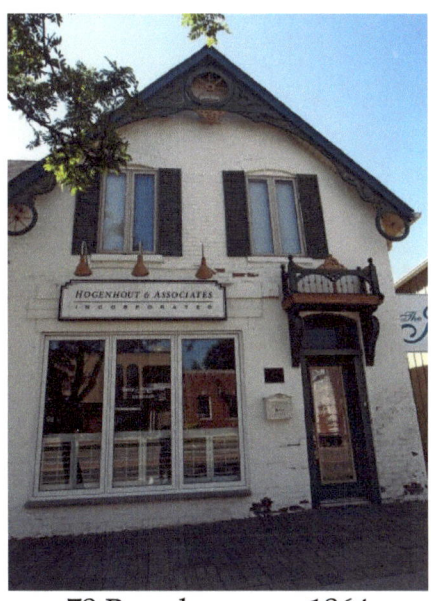

78 Broadway – c. 1864
Gothic Revival with steeply pitched roof, decorative
bargeboard in the façade gable

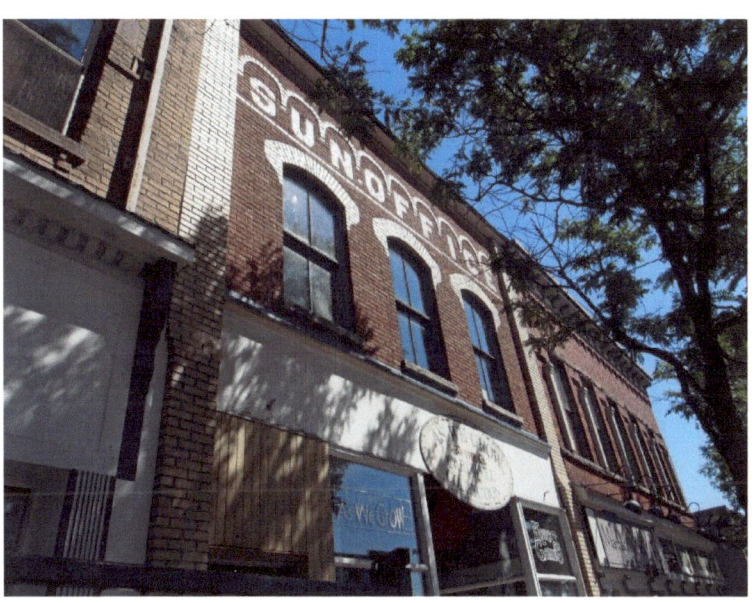

113 Broadway

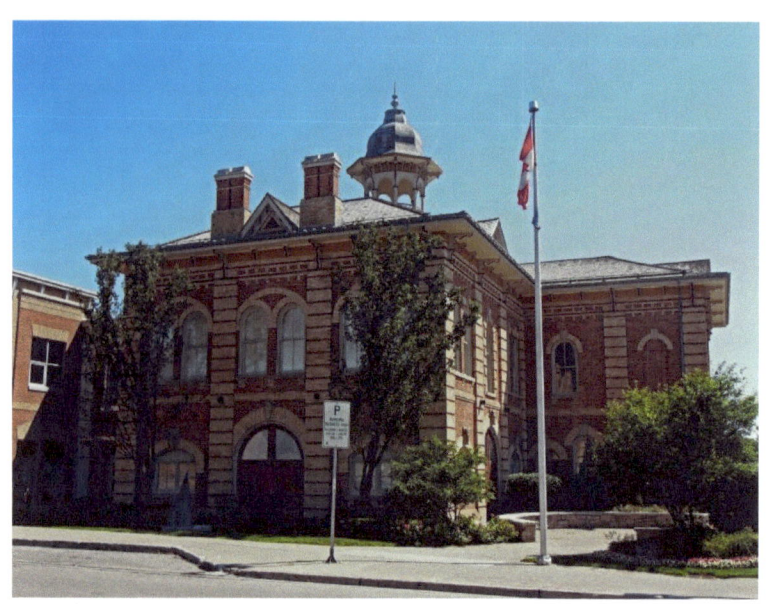

87 Broadway – Orangeville Town Hall – built to serve as town hall, municipal offices, market area, opera house – c. 1875 Italianate architecture with projecting roof eaves, paired cornice brackets, pedimented roof line, and use of contrasting brick colours – the cupola is a prominent feature

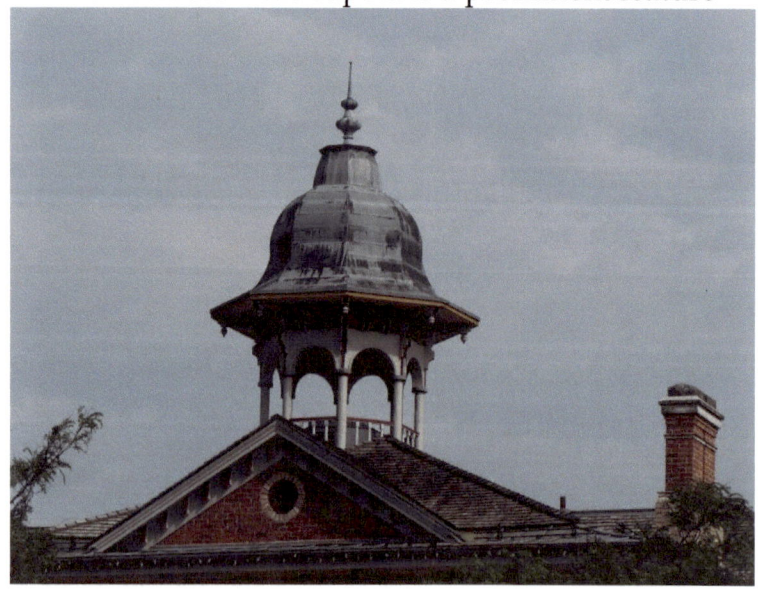

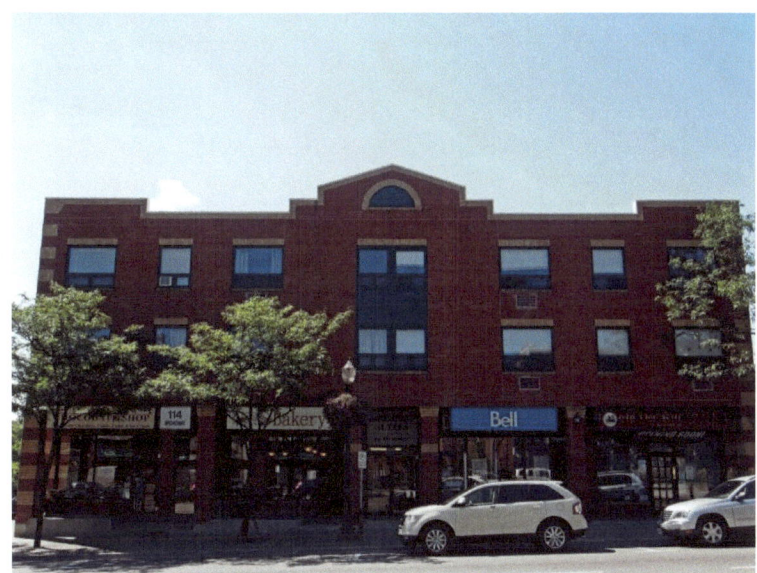

114 Broadway

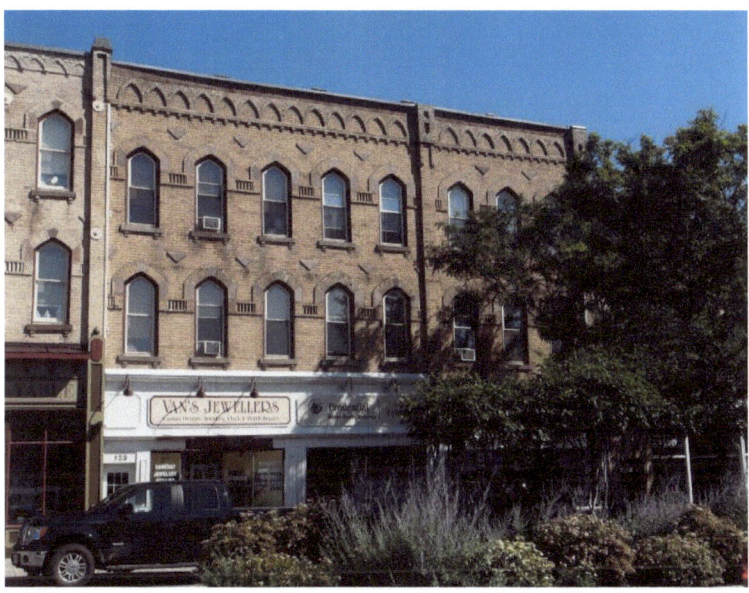

117-123 Broadway – Italianate style with buff coloured brick, pointed windows with keystones of brown locally quarried sandstone, cornice with raised brick pattern using dentils and arches

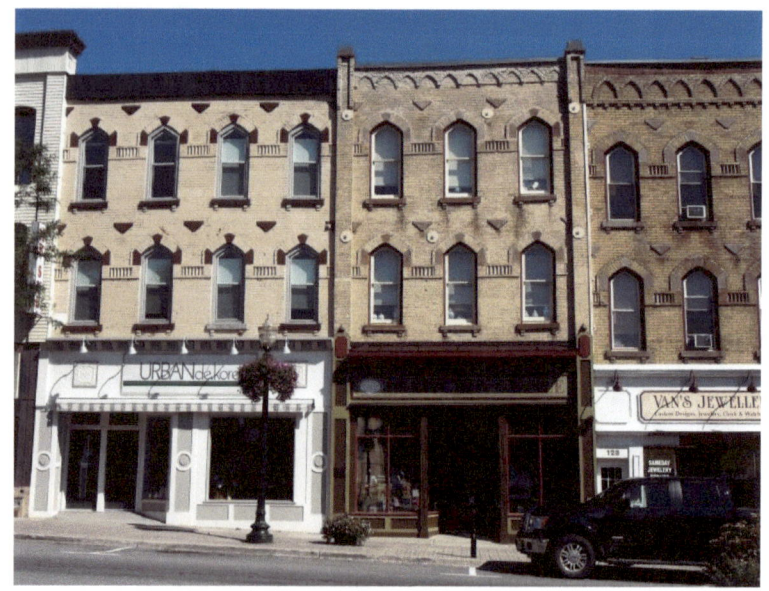

123-127 Broadway

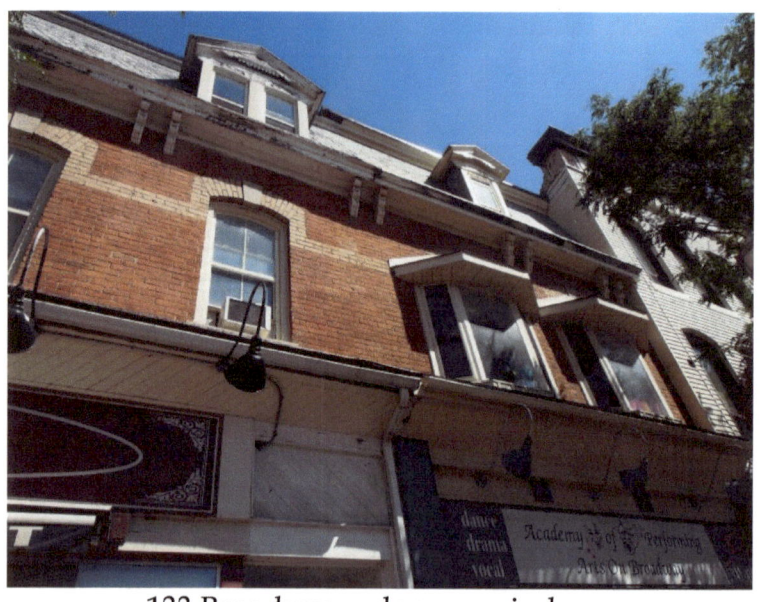

133 Broadway – dormer windows

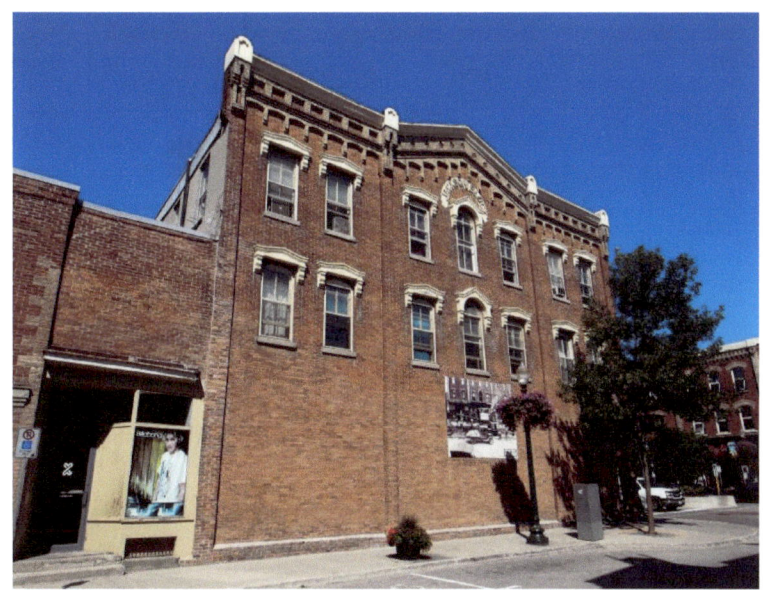

148 Broadway – Jackson Block – Italianate – built between 1874 and 1875 (Thomas Jackson, saddler) – elaborate raised window hoods and lintels over the windows, red brick pilasters divide the façade into three bays, buff brick bracket at roofline, elaborate red and buff brick corbelled cornice tops the structure, pedimented roofline over the central bays

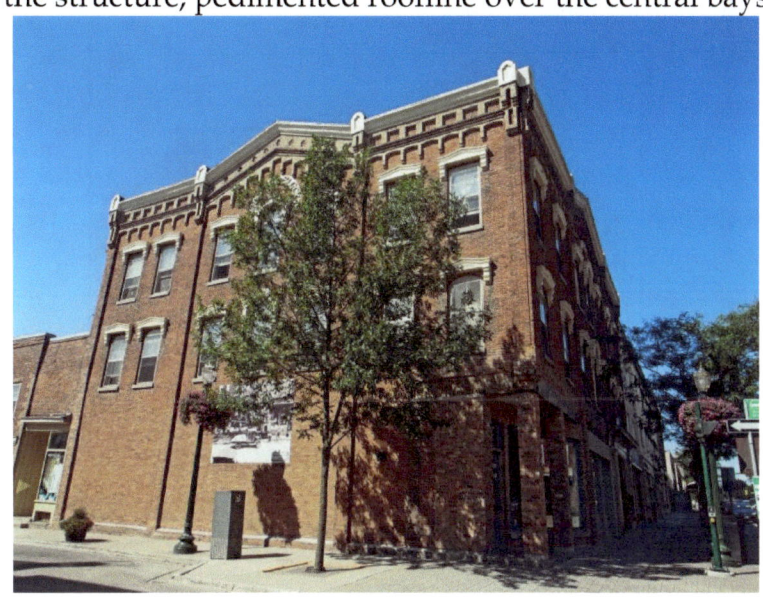

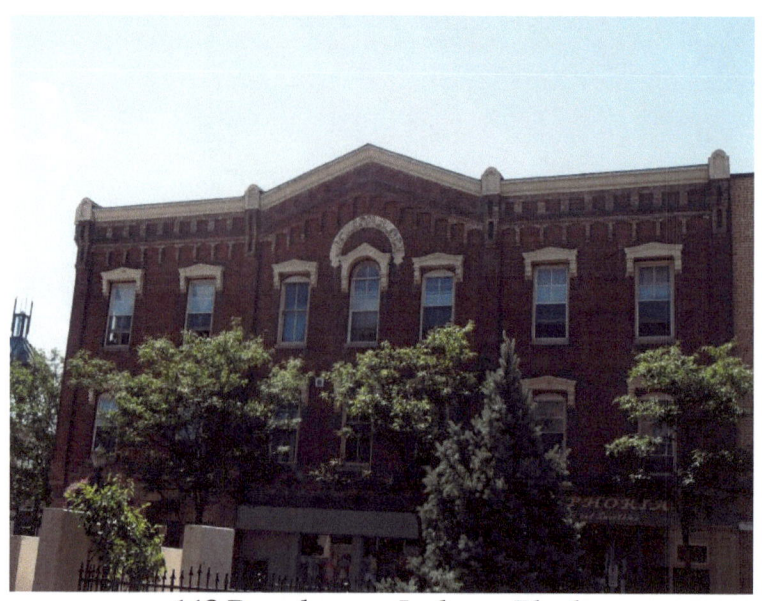

148 Broadway – Jackson Block

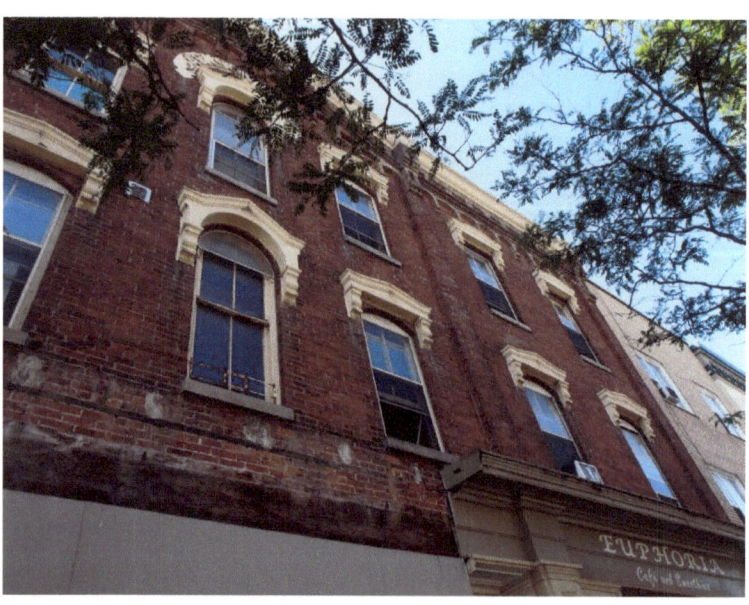

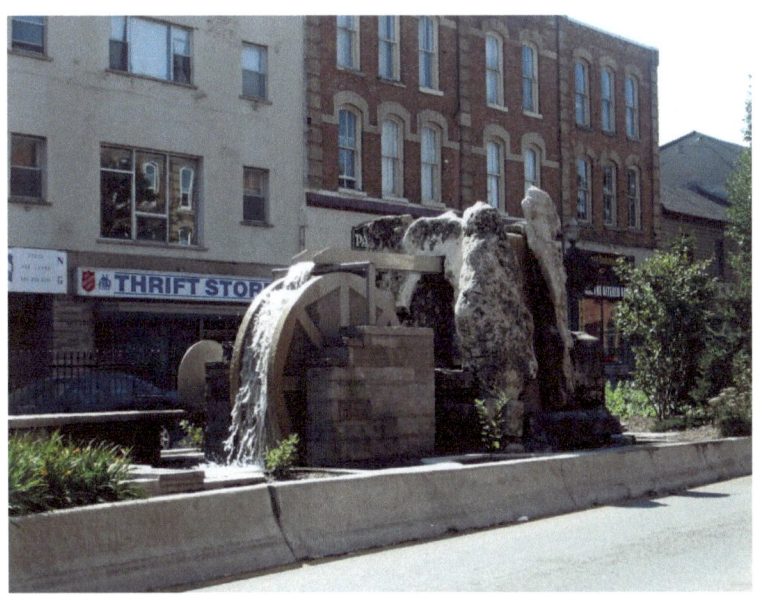

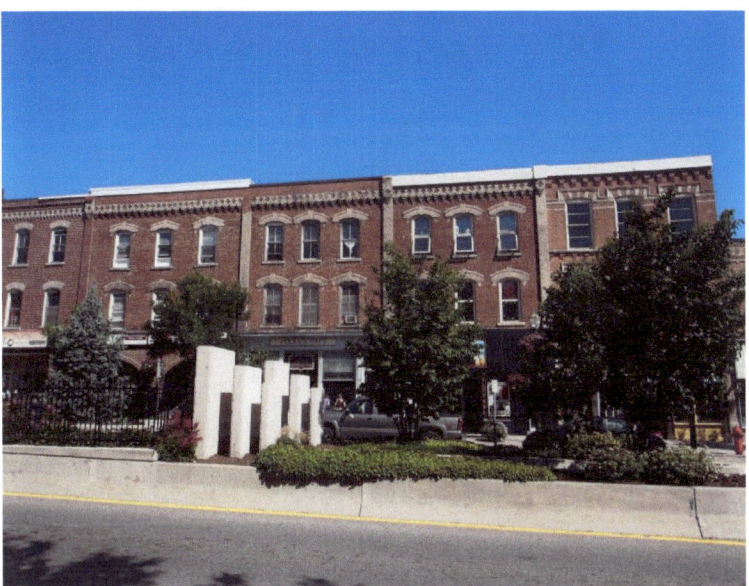

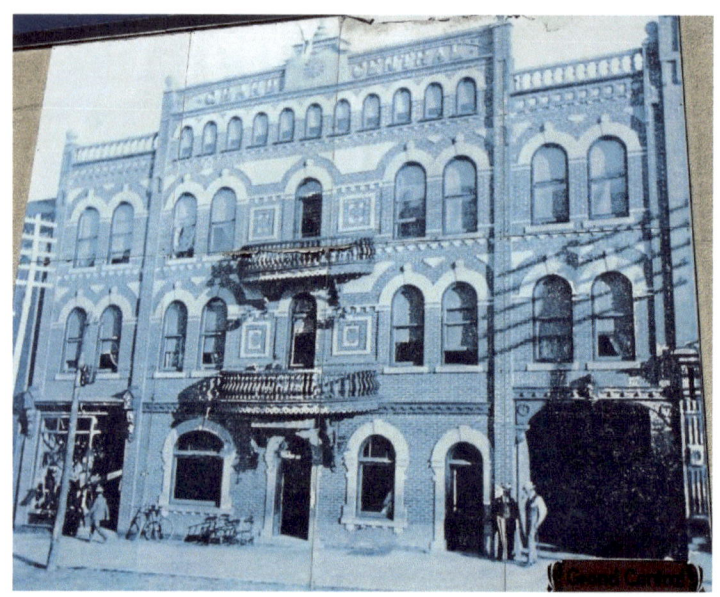

Mural of Grand Central Hotel

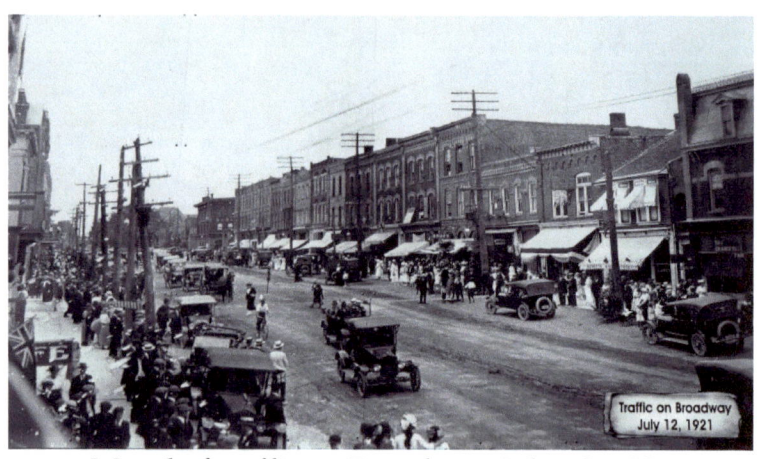

Mural of traffic on Broadway July 12, 1921

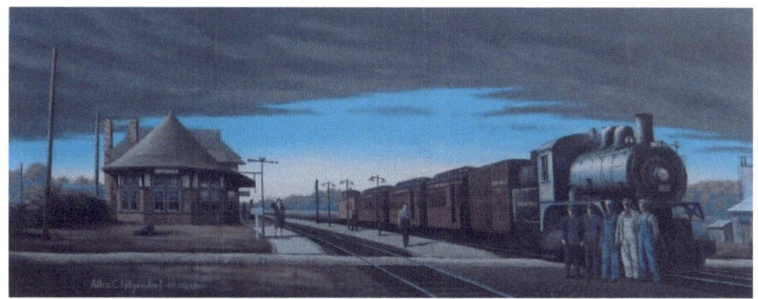

Mural

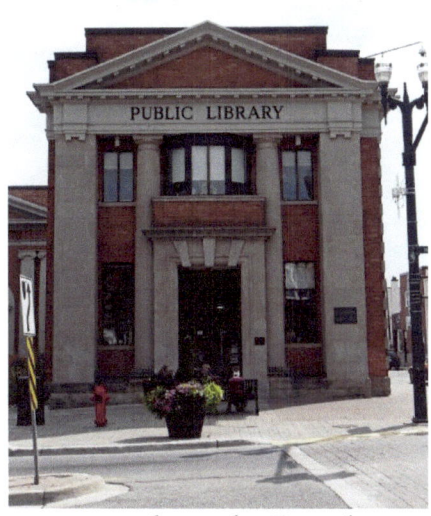

The decorative stonework on the Broadway and Mill Street facades is a hallmark of the Beaux-Arts Classicism style with the use of columns

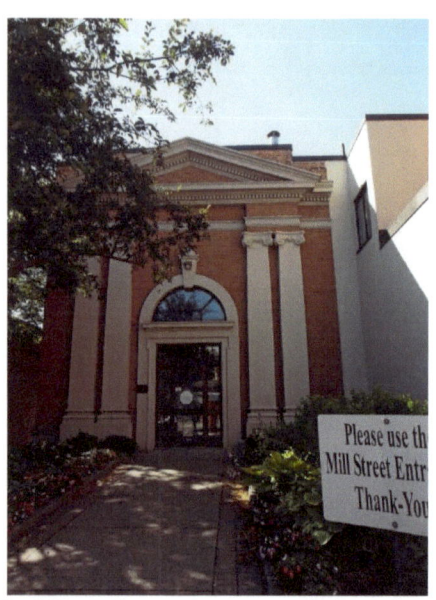

Orangeville Public Library recessed façade on Broadway

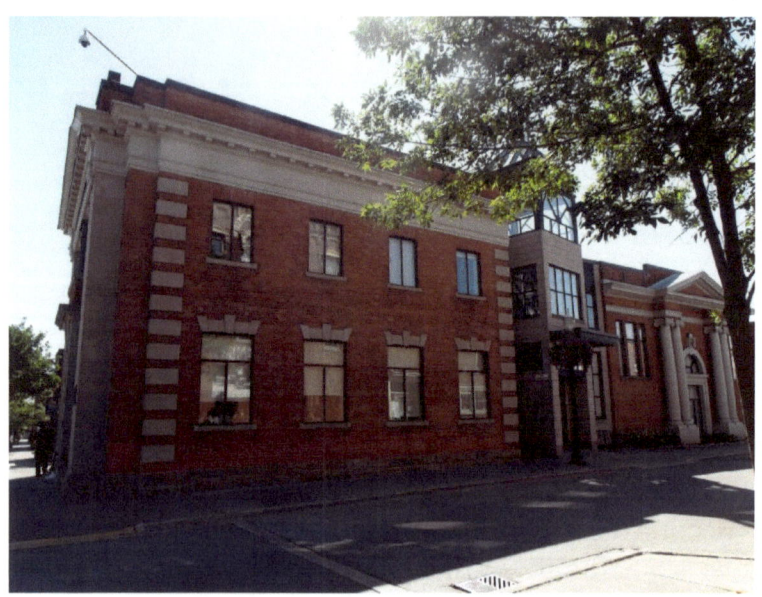

Orangeville Public Library 1907 – 1 Mill Street

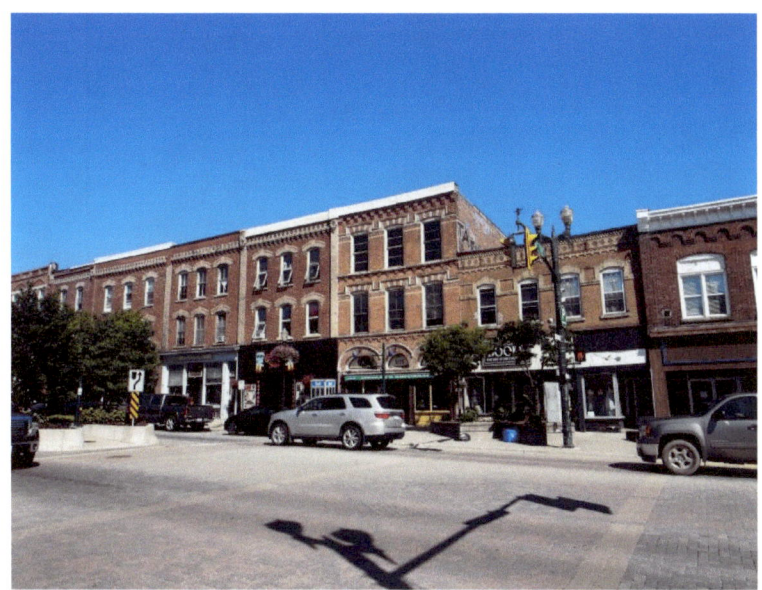

153 Broadway c. 1876 – Italianate style – white limestone details enhancing the façade, dentil brick pattern across the roofline and repeated under the continuous limestone sills running under the windows on each storey

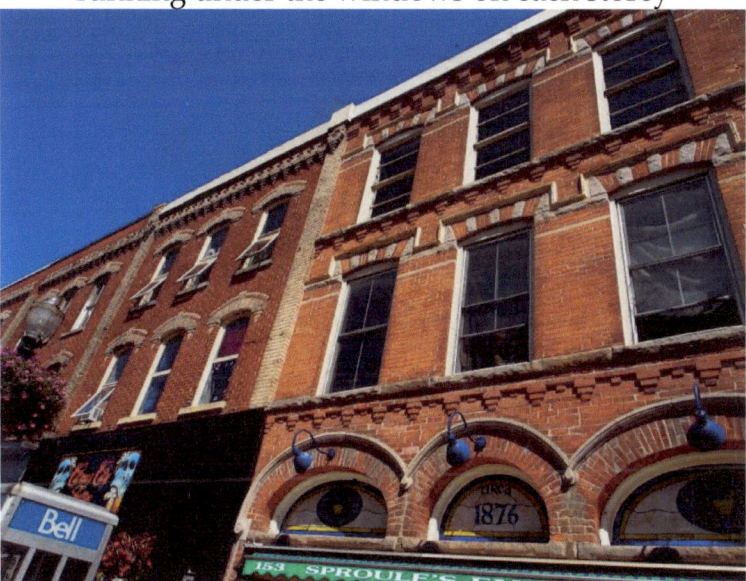

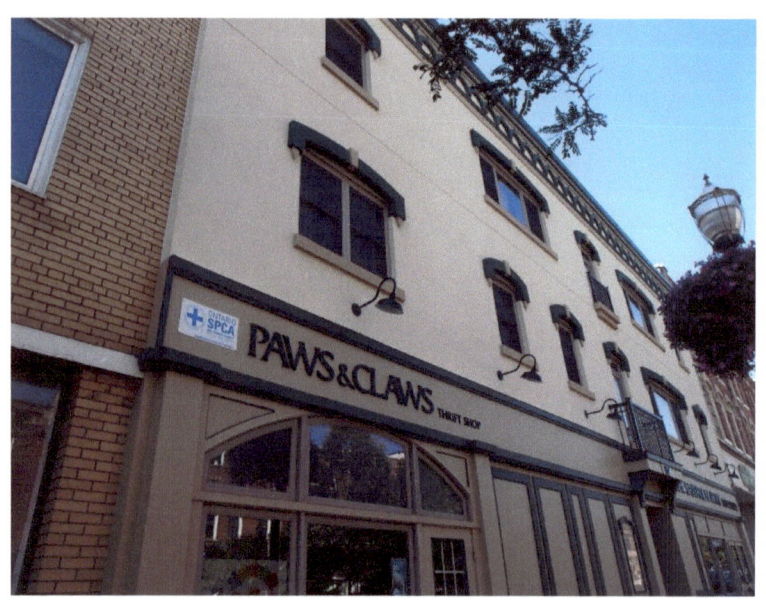

162 Broadway

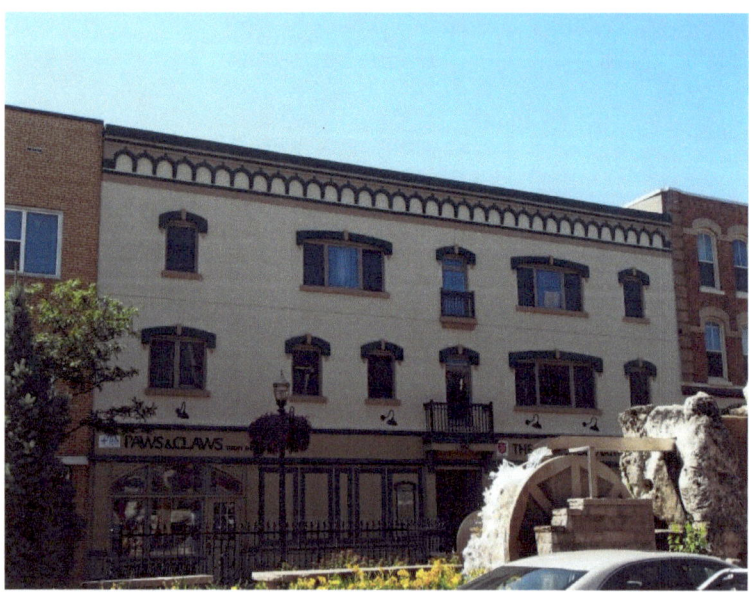

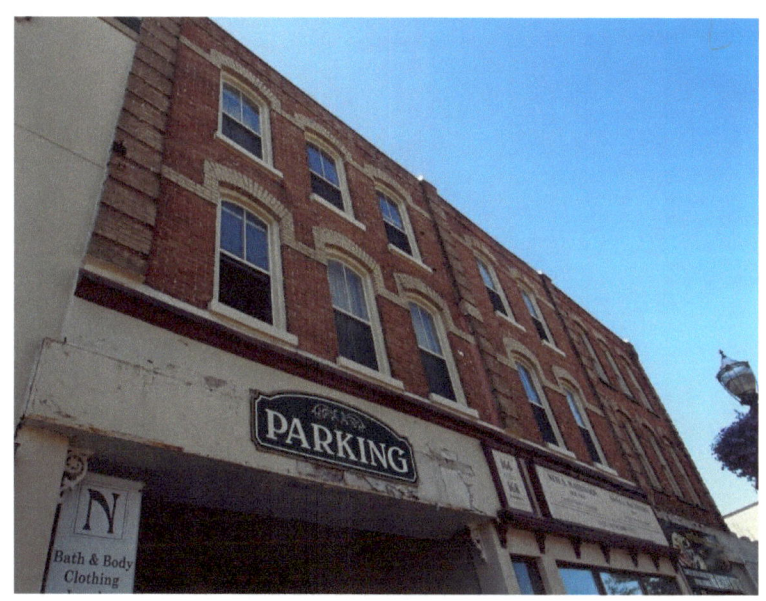

166-168 Broadway

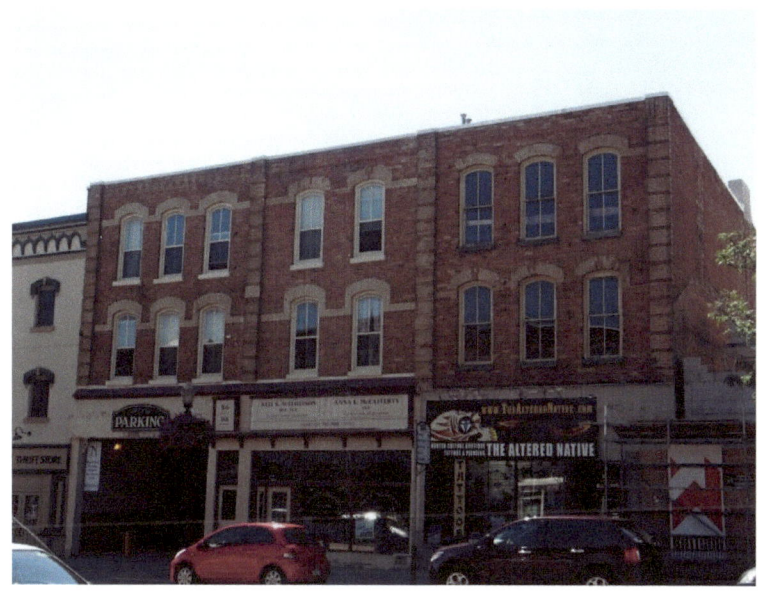

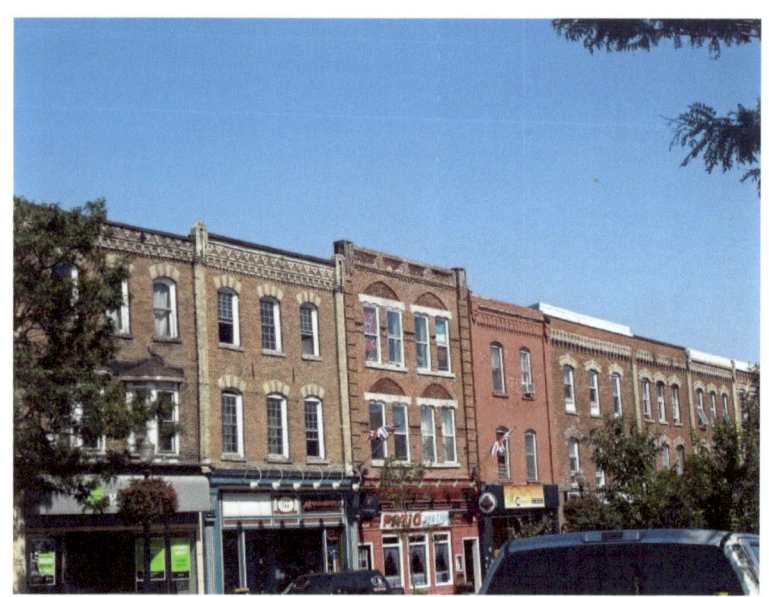

165-179 Broadway

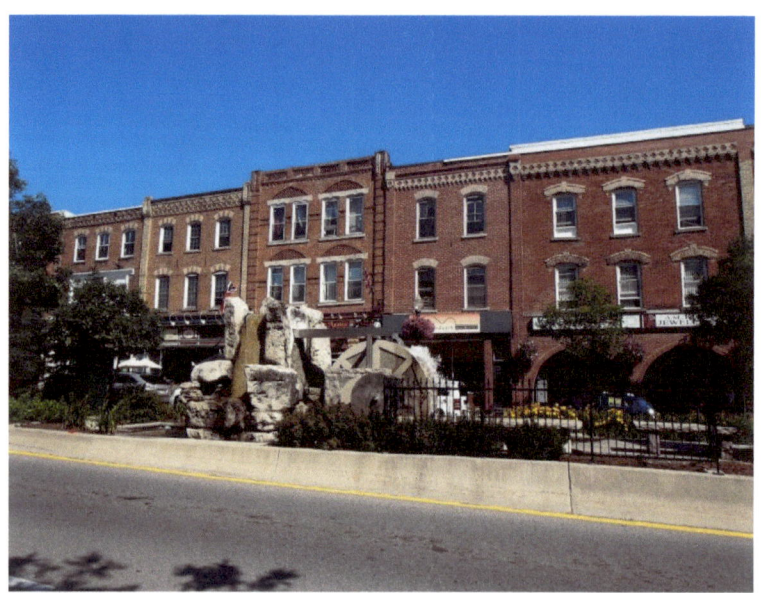

177 Broadway

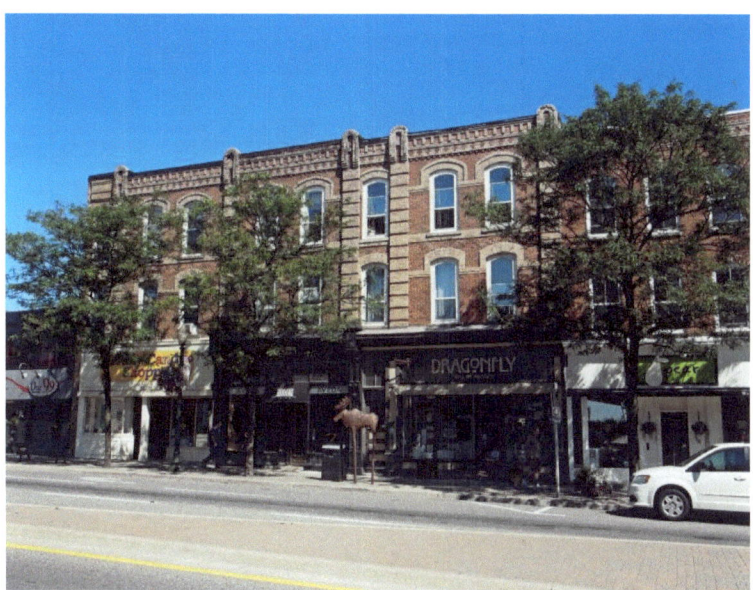

187-195 Broadway – Italianate – constructed for Mary Ketchum – upper floors with five-course buff brick banding, voussoirs are buff brick with a decorative raised edge, the pilasters are quoined in buff brick ending in a round topped brick design above the roof line.

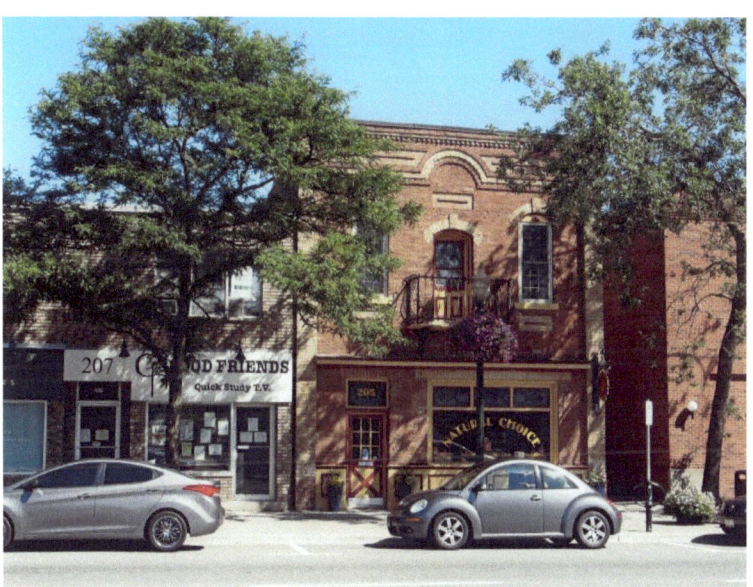

205-207 Broadway – Italianate – decorative brickwork, second-storey door

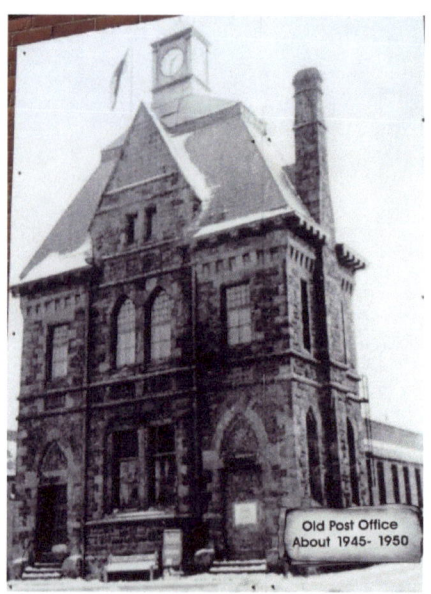

Old Post Office – 216 Broadway – Chateau style
Two storey, built of limestone quarried in the Hockley Valley, steeply
pitched roof

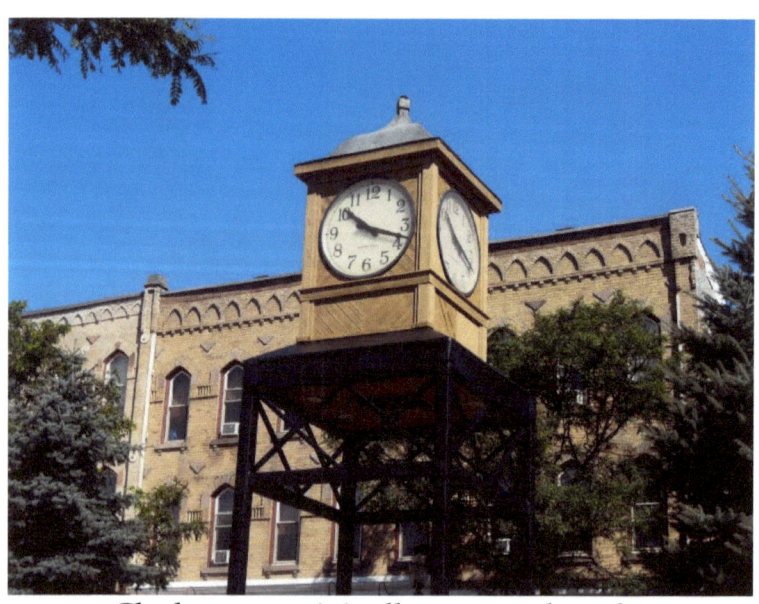

Clock tower originally mounted on the
old Post Office building

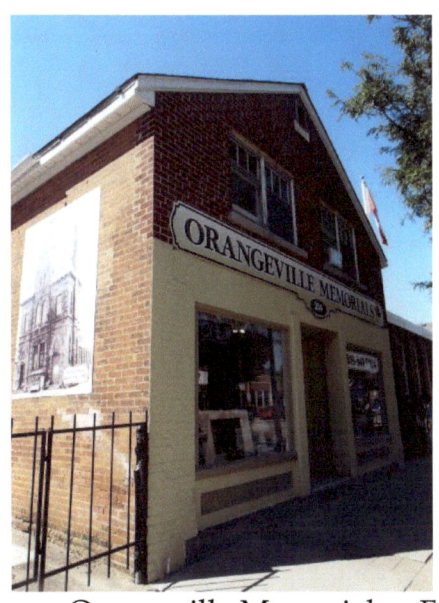

214 Broadway – Orangeville Memorials – Frontier style

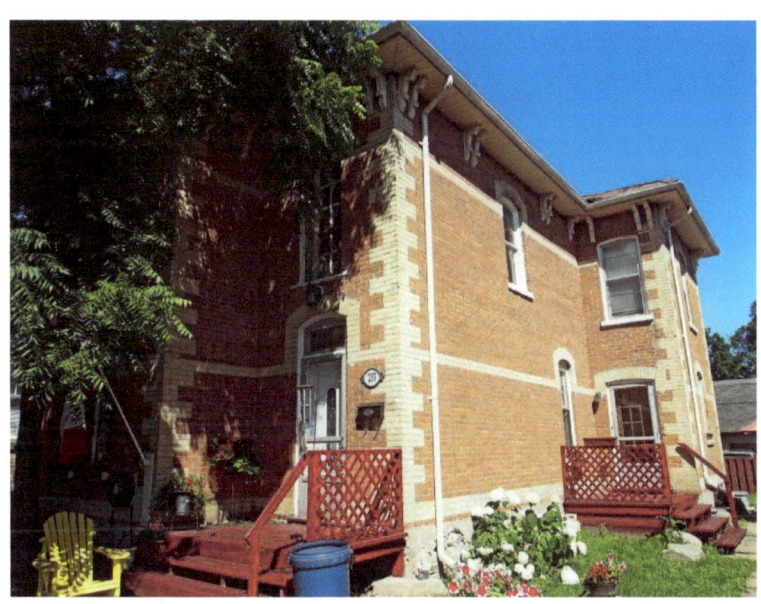

237 Broadway – Italianate – dichromatic brickwork,
paired cornice brackets

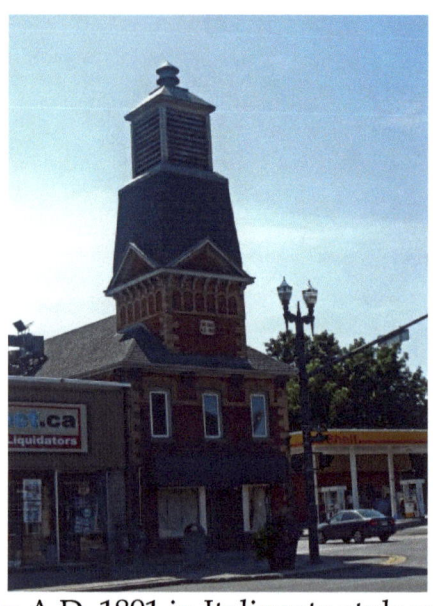

Fire Hall built in A.D. 1891 in Italianate style with the original hose tower being 62 feet high and a 20,000-gallon reservoir located beneath the building. The fire bell sounded a 9 p.m. curfew for anyone under 16.

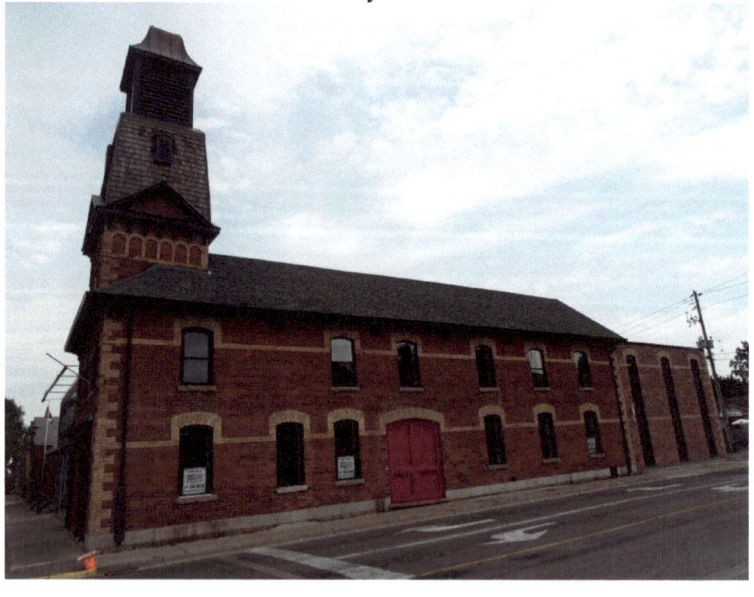

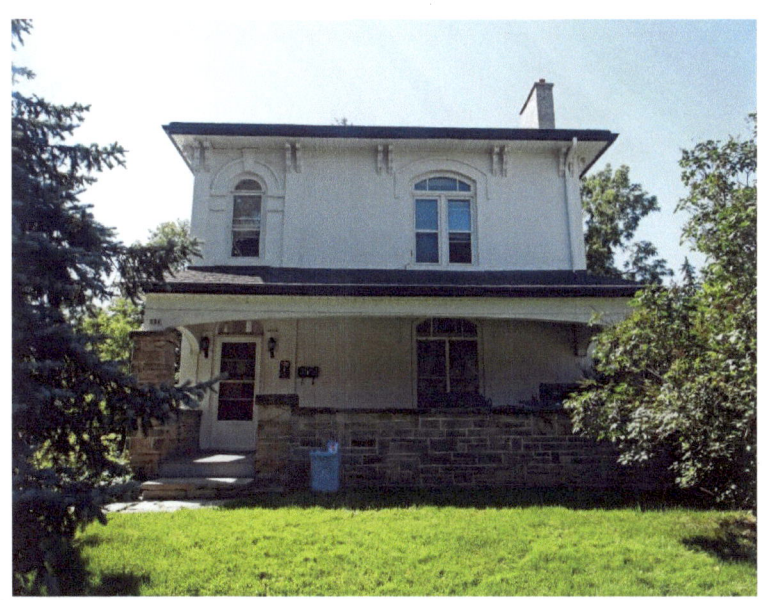

236 Broadway – two storey – Broadway Animal Hospital
Italianate style c. 1890s – home of Andrew Dods

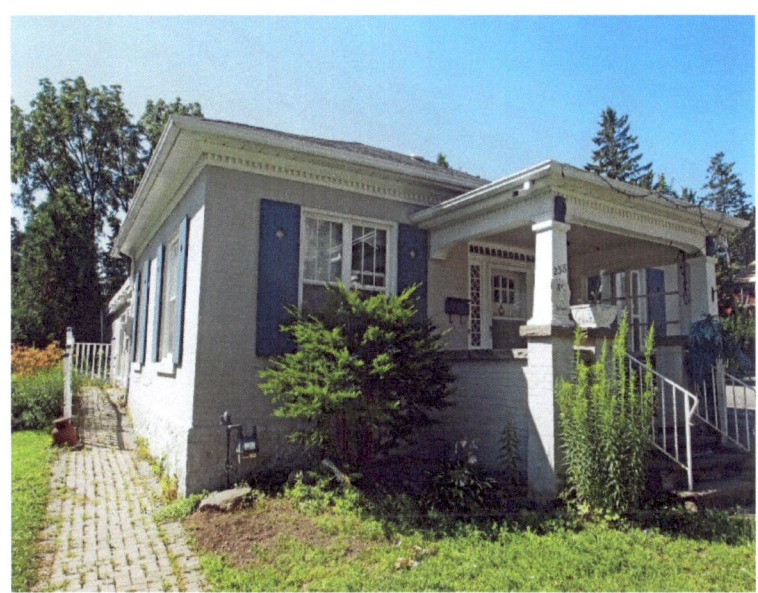

238 Broadway – Regency Cottage – one-storey, low-pitched
hip roof, symmetrical front façade

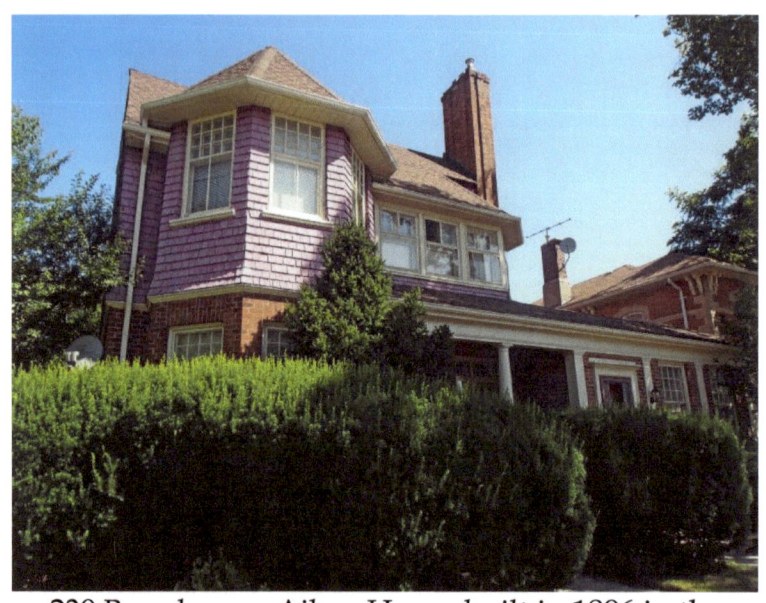

239 Broadway – Aiken House built in 1896 in the Queen Anne style – turret, gambrel roof, chimney with vertical pilaster-like brick work detail

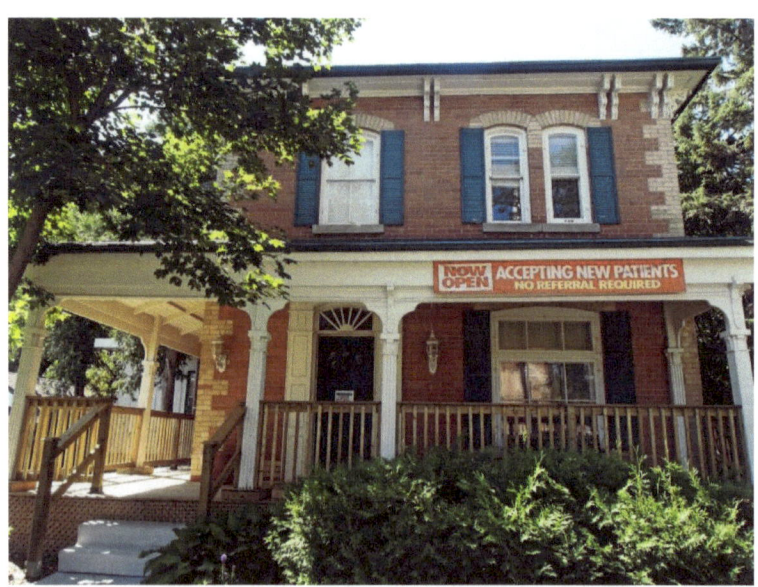

240 Broadway – Italianate – paired cornice brackets, dichromatic brickwork, wrap-around veranda

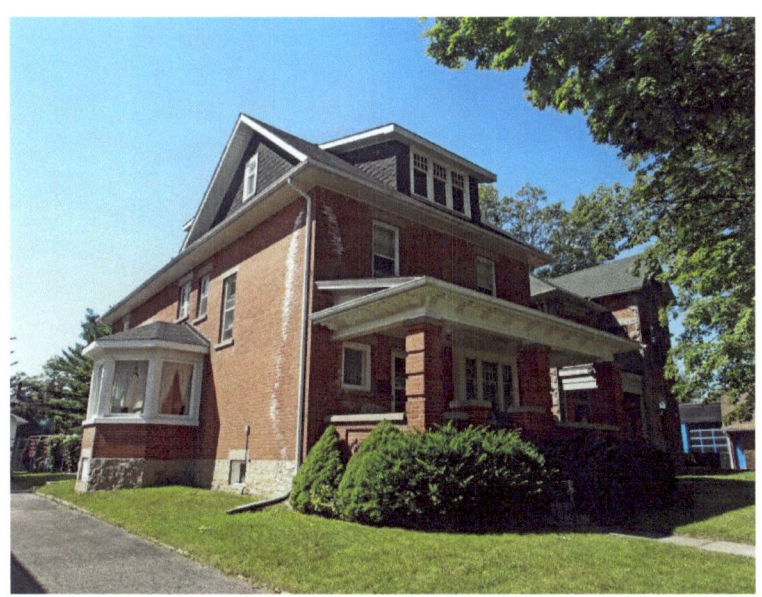

248 Broadway – Italianate – single cornice brackets remain on porch, dormer in the attic

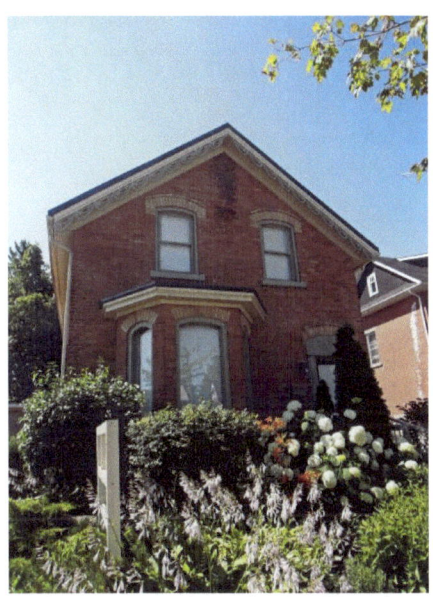

Broadway – Gothic Revival style, buff-coloured voussoirs, ornamental vergeboards hanging from the roof on the gable

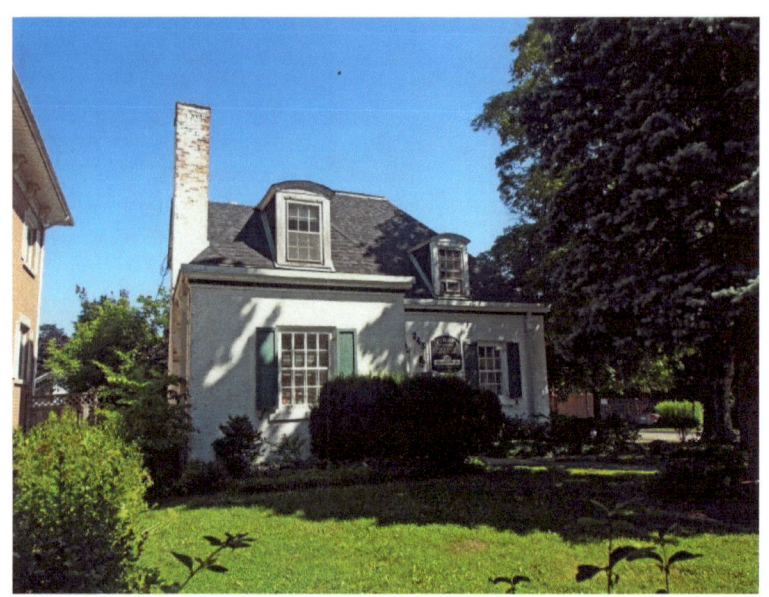

243 Broadway – 1½ storey with dormers in the attic

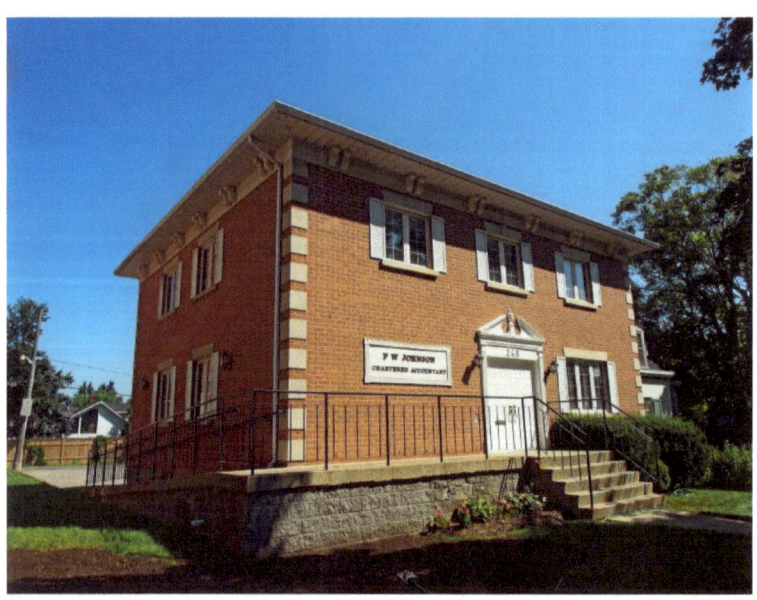

245 Broadway – Italianate style – paired cornice brackets, dichromatic brickwork

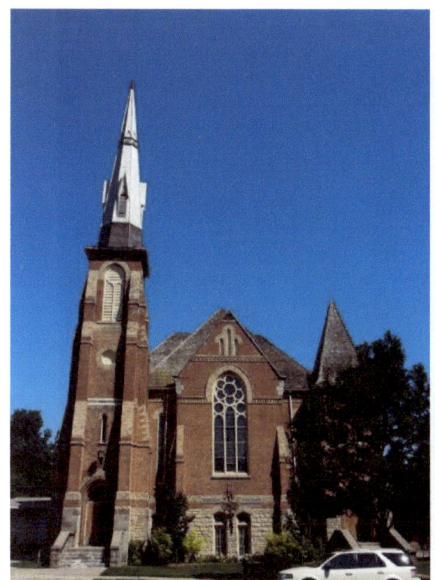
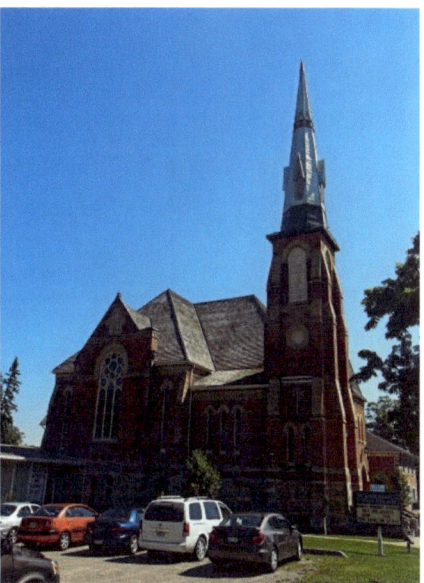

247 Broadway – Westminster United Church built in 1879 – originally Zion Presbyterian Church – Victorian Gothic Revival with a spire at the top finial to act as a lightning rod, lancet windows, steeply pitched roof lines, buttresses to strengthen the walls

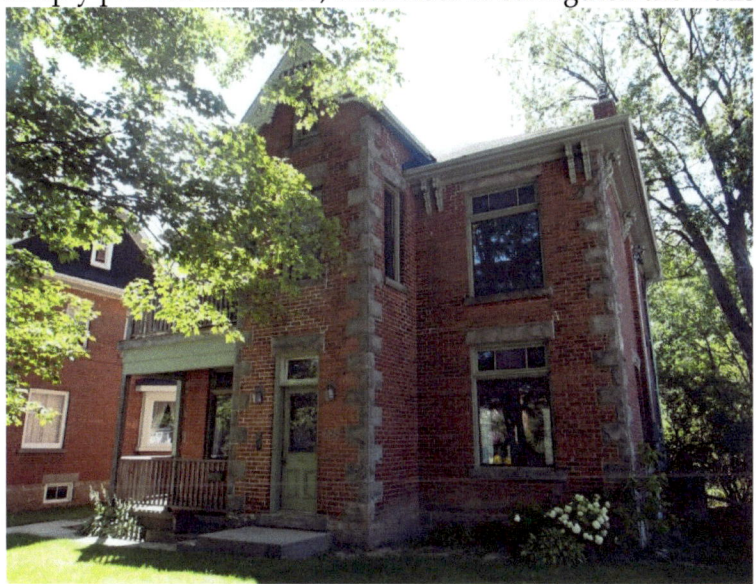

250 Broadway – Italianate – quoining on the corners, paired cornice brackets

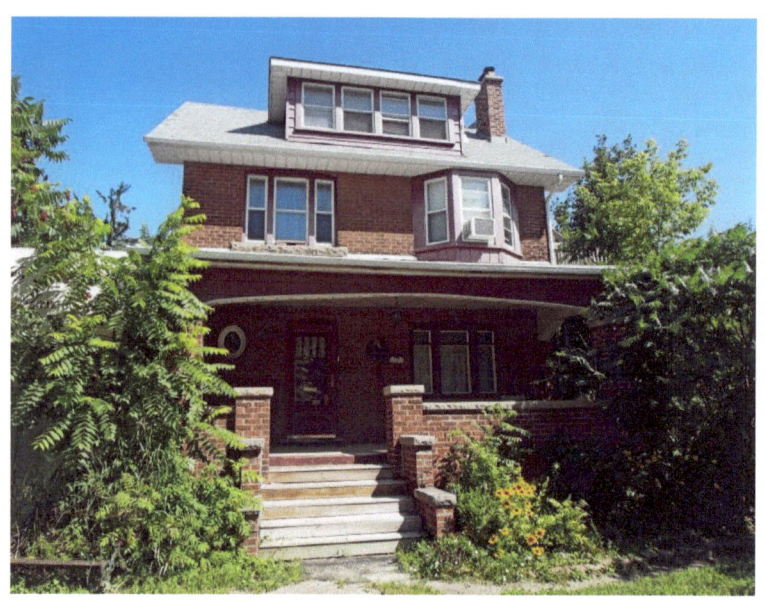

253 Broadway – dormer in attic

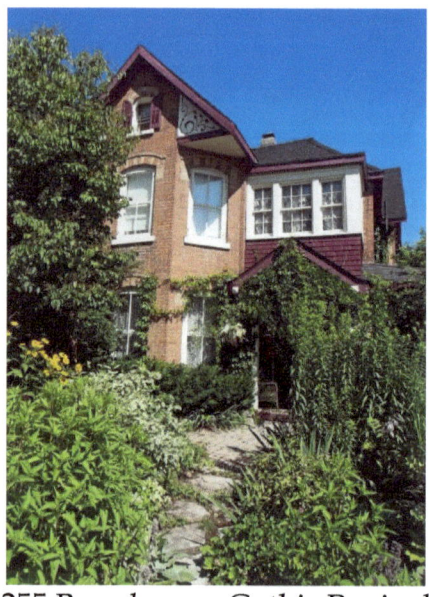

255 Broadway – Gothic Revival

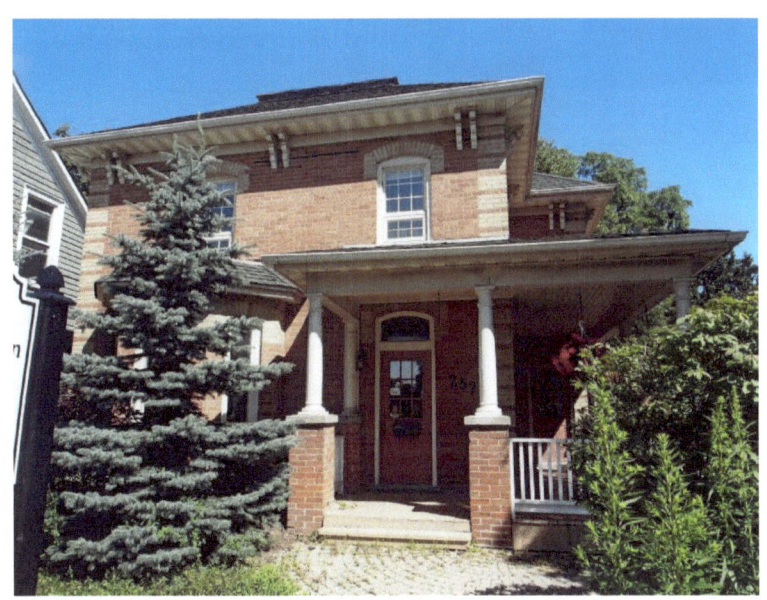

257 Broadway – Italianate – wrap-around verandah, paired cornice brackets

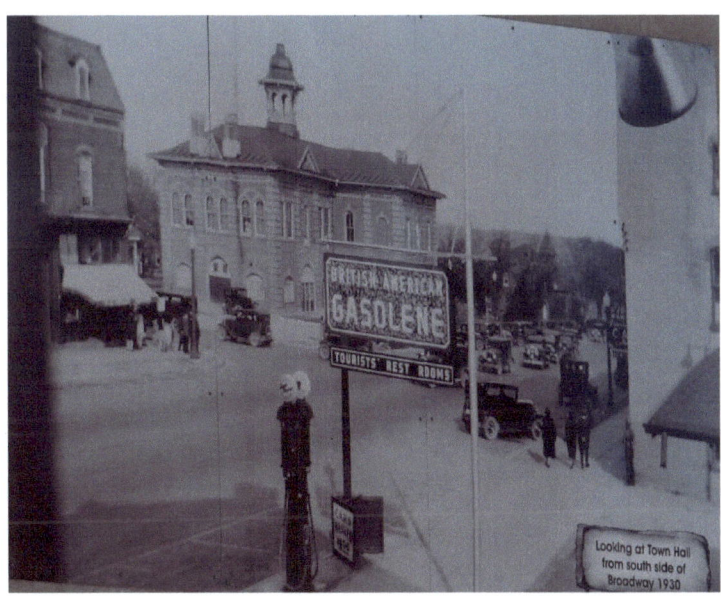

Mural looking at Town Hall from south side of Broadway in 1930

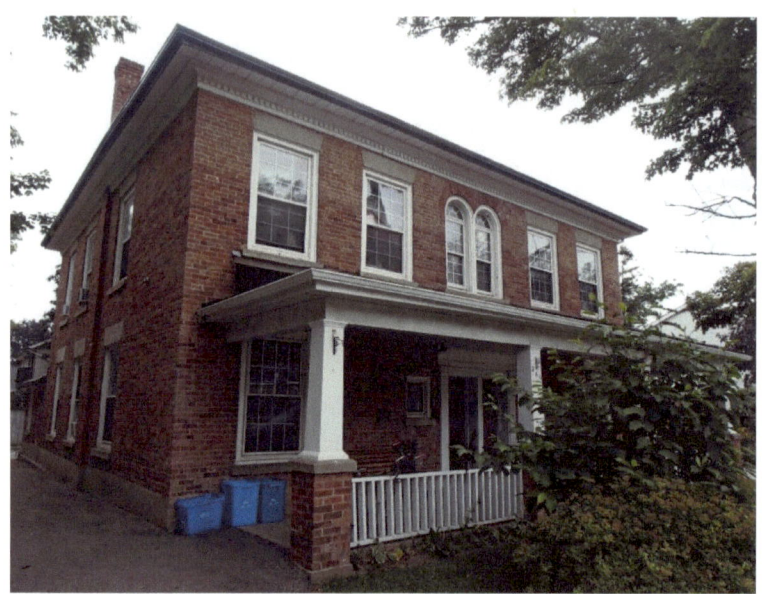

260 Broadway – Irish Georgian style built in 1858 by Guy Leslie, an Irish immigrant – features a hip roof, central door and a balanced arrangement of windows with a pair of round top windows grouped together on the second floor. It became known as "Castle Leslie" by the locals.

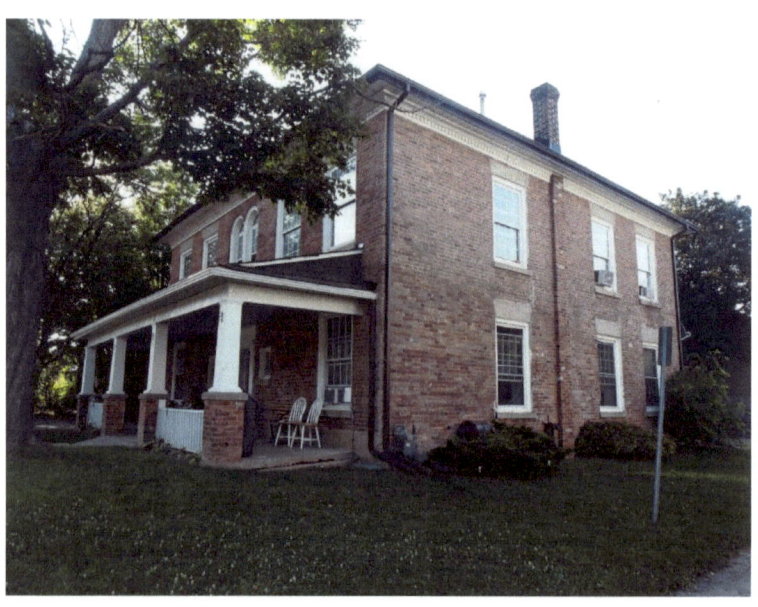

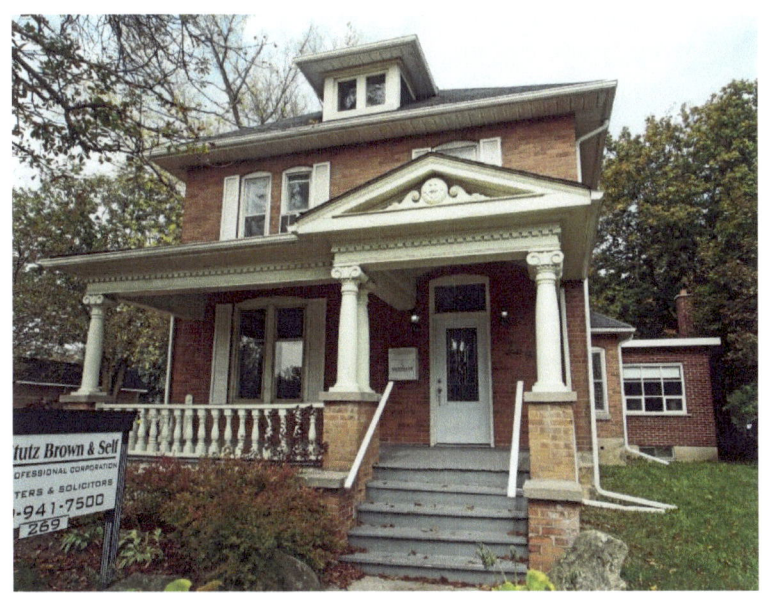

269 Broadway – Italianate – wide porch

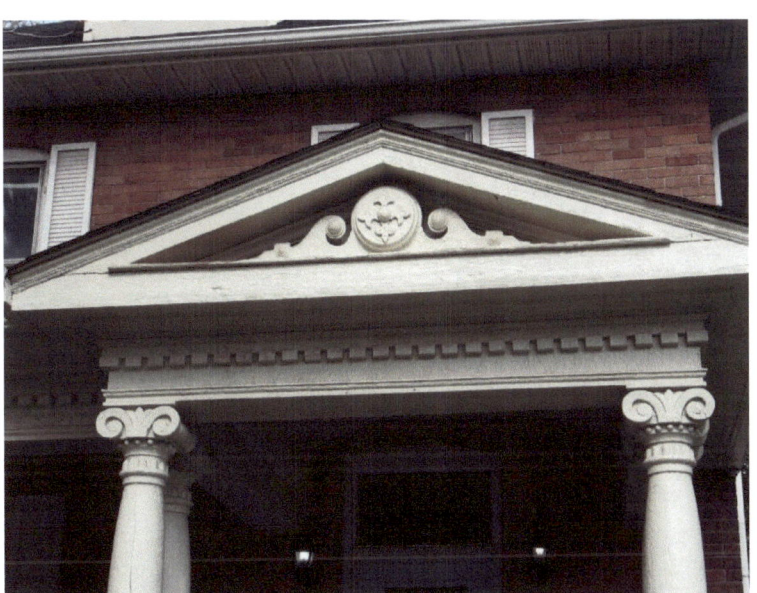

pediment (low gable over the door) with decorated tympanum, decorative capitals on the pillars

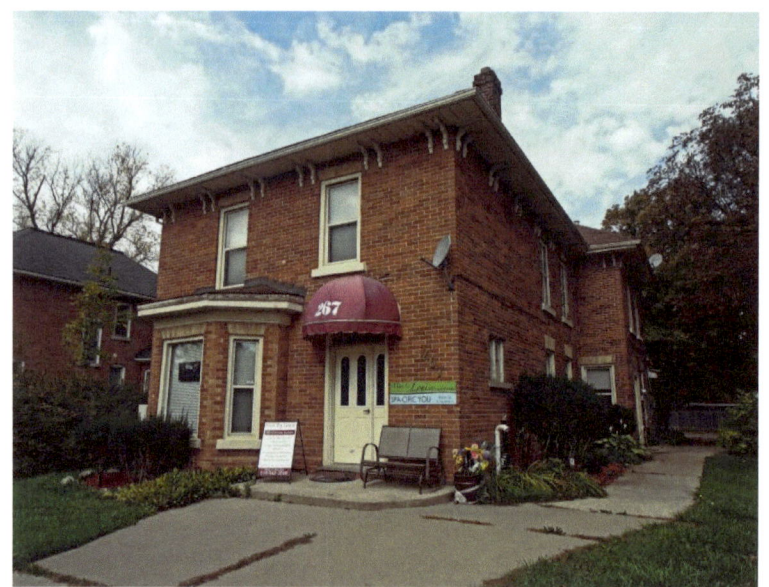

267 Broadway – Italianate – paired cornice brackets, bay window

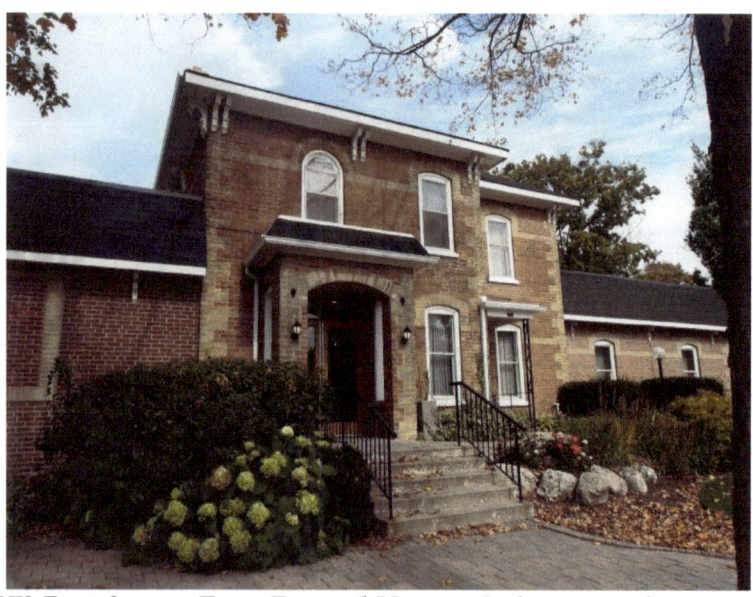

273 Broadway – Egan Funeral Home – Italianate style, paired cornice brackets, dichromatic brickwork, rounded window openings

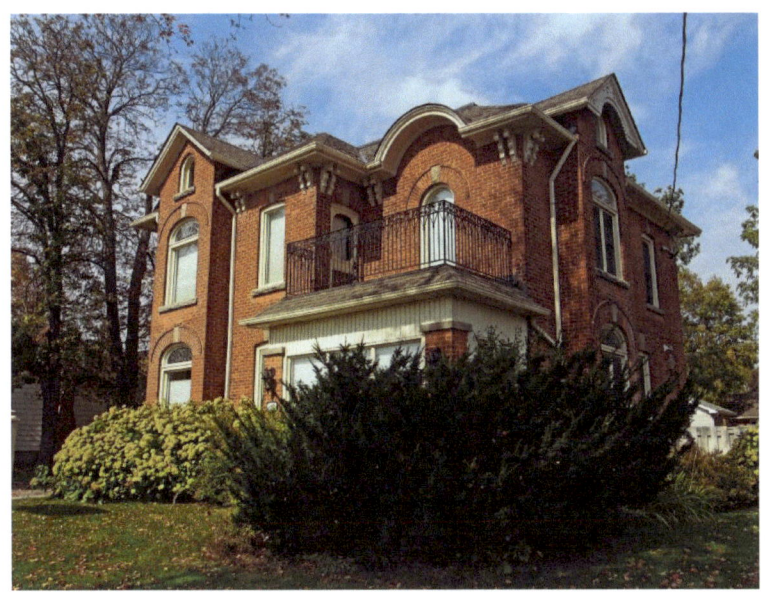

283 Broadway – Romanesque – massive shape, tower on side and front, large arches over windows

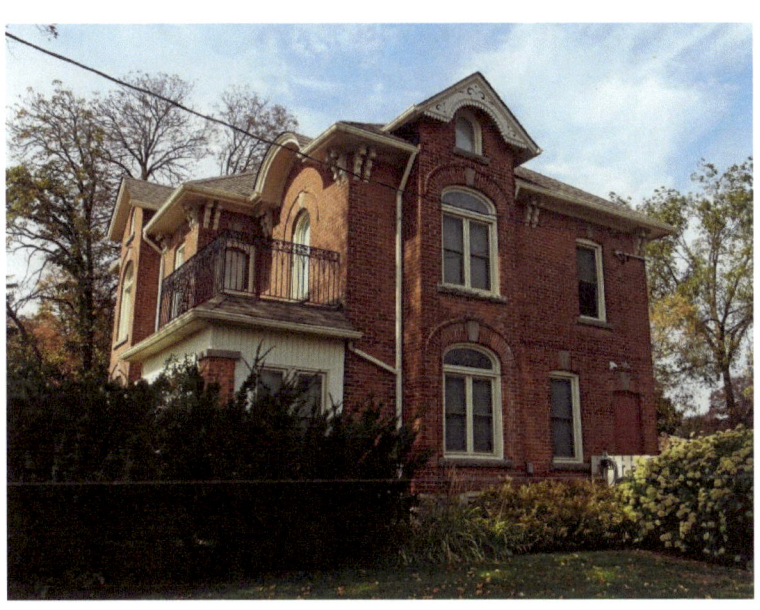

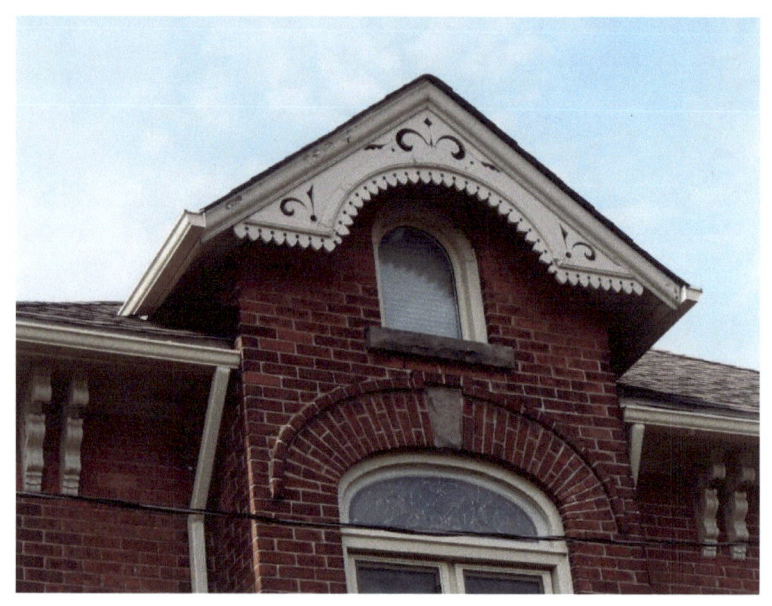

283 Broadway – detail – decorative Vergeboard, paired cornice brackets

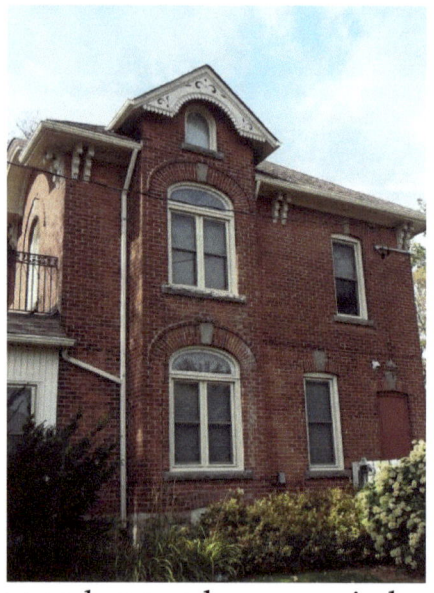

Tower, large arches over windows

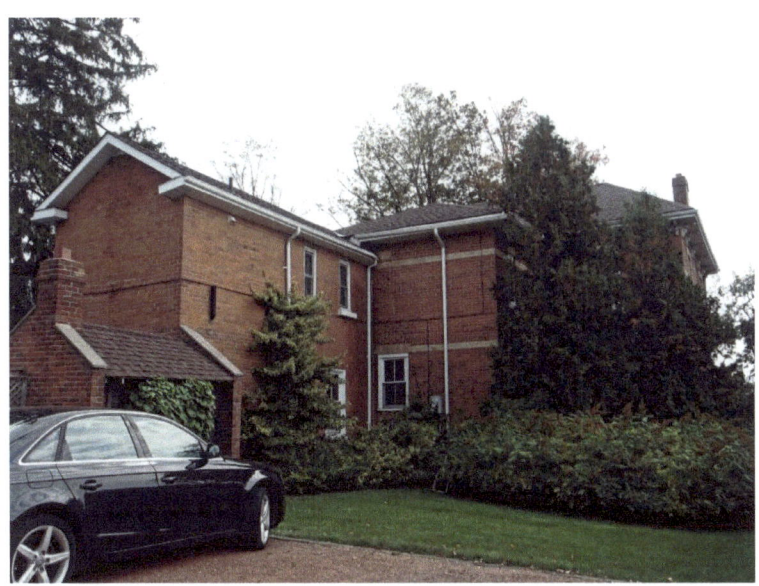

283 Broadway from rear – a huge house

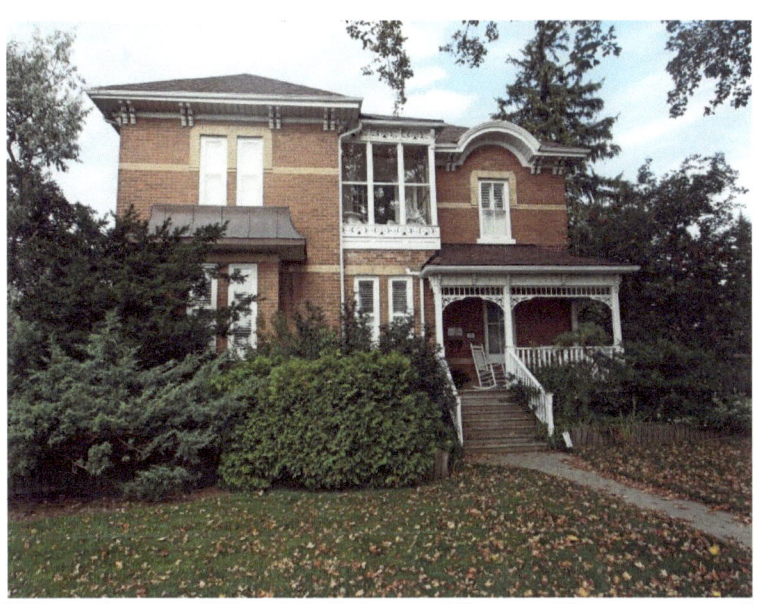

277 Broadway – Ellen McCabe and James Thompson, tailor
c. 1879 - Italianate

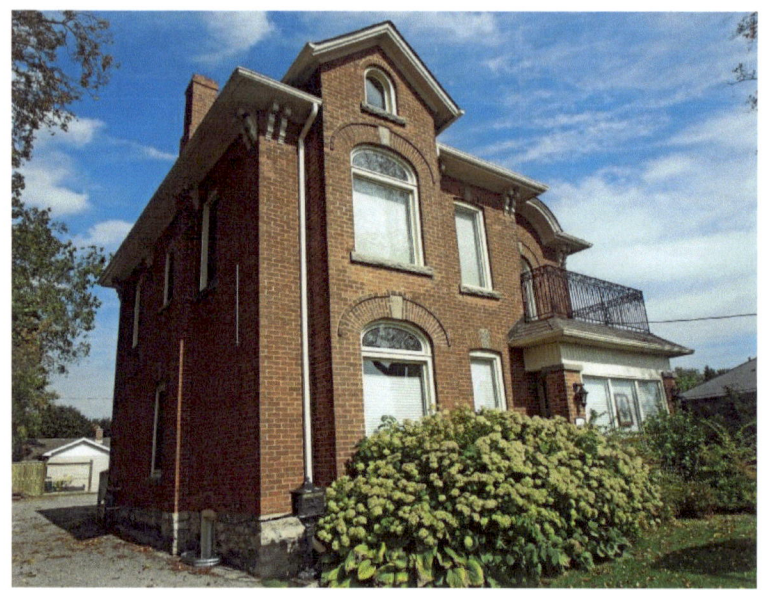

287 Broadway – Romanesque – tower, large arches over windows, paired cornice brackets, iron cresting

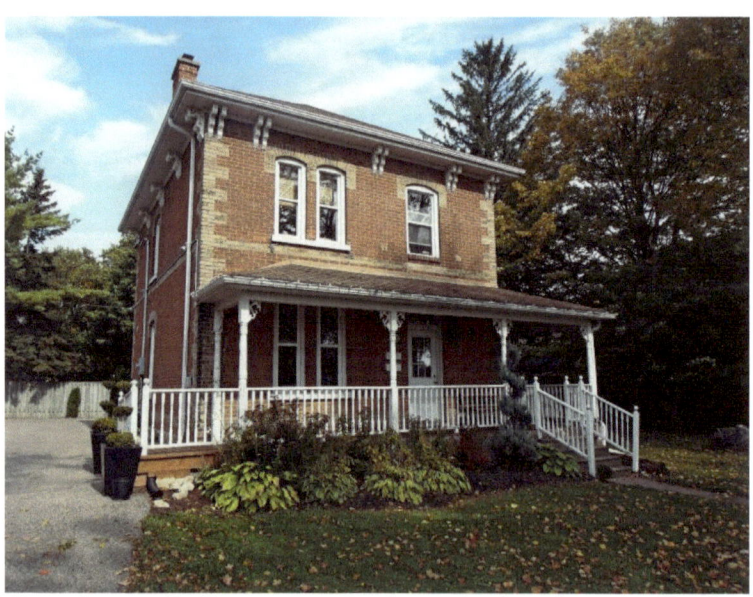

293 Broadway – Italianate – paired cornice brackets, buff coloured soldiering over windows, buff coloured quoining on corners

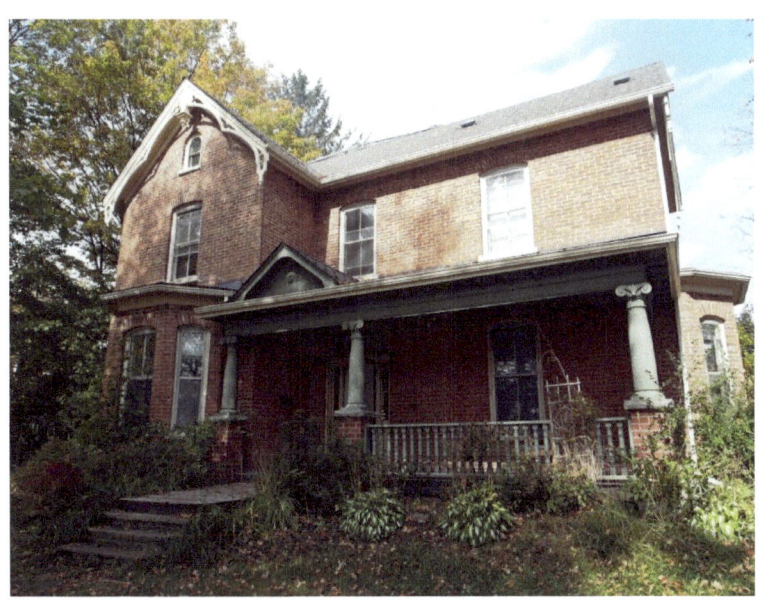

291 Broadway – Gothic Revival – pediment over doorway, bay window

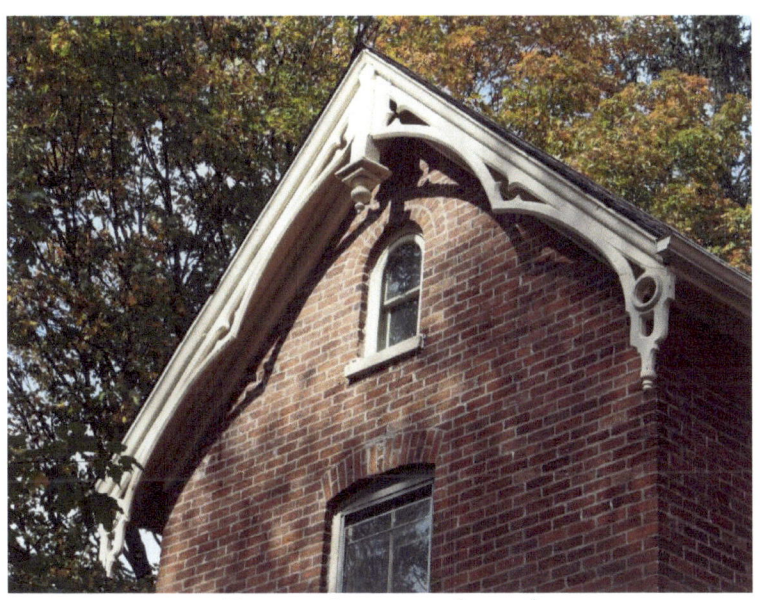

Decorative vergeboard

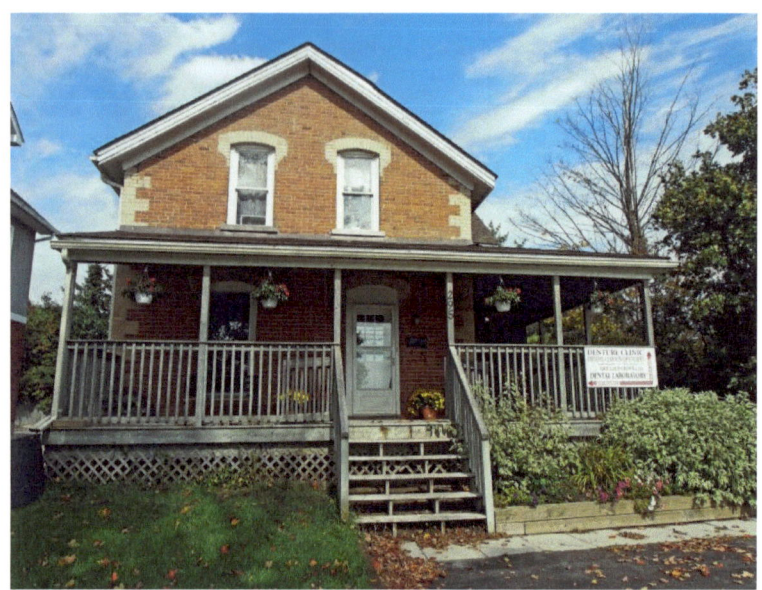

295 Broadway – Gothic Revival – buff soldiering over windows, and buff brick quoining on corners

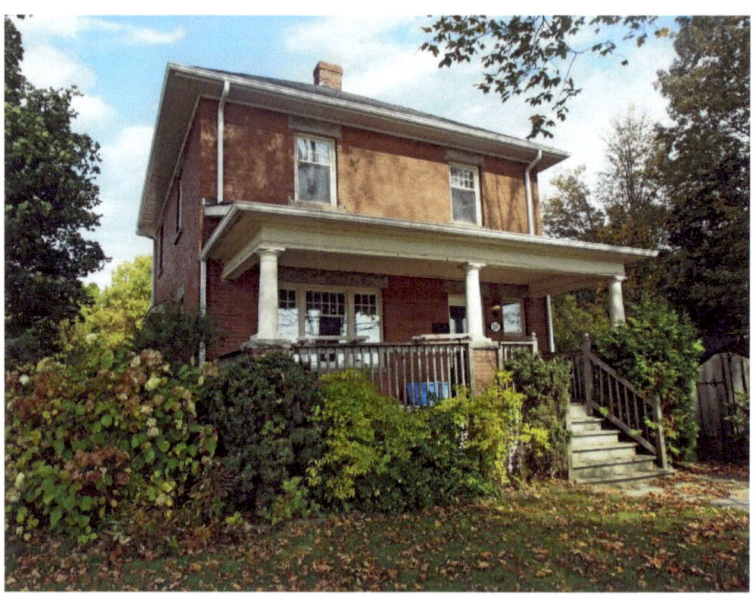

297 Broadway – Italianate – wide porch, stone lintels above and below windows

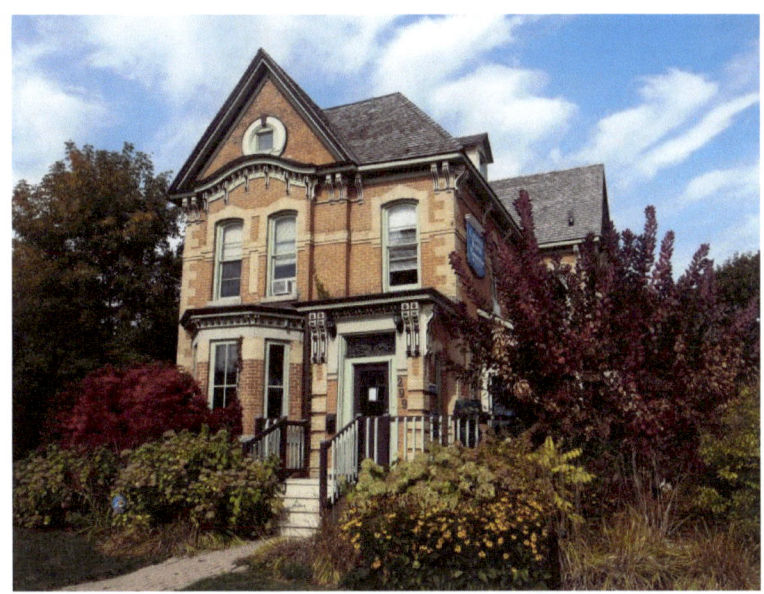

299 Broadway – Gothic Revival – sharply pitched gables, dichromatic brickwork, decorative cornice brackets, bay window, dormer in attic

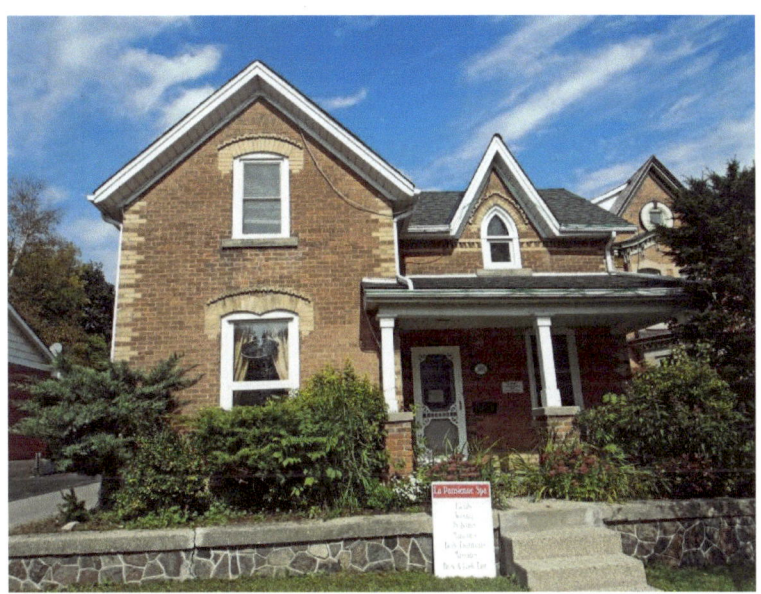

301 Broadway – William and Jane Hall, retired farmer c. 1881 Gothic Revival – dichromatic brickwork

Architectural Terms

Brackets: a decorative or weight-bearing structural element which forms a right angle with one side against a wall and the other under a projecting surface such as an eave or roof. Example: 236 Broadway	
Buttress: a masonry structure built against or projecting from a wall which serves to support or reinforce the wall. In Canadian architecture, they are sometimes used for decoration. Example: 247 Broadway, Westminster United Church	
Cornice: originally the wooden overhang of the roof. With the use of stone, brick, iron and steel, the cornice is any projecting shelf at the top of a ceiling or roof. They can be very decorative. Example: 257 Broadway	
Cupola: a small, dome-like structure on top of a building often used to provide a lookout or to admit light and air. Example: 87 Broadway (Town Hall)	
Dentil Moulding: an even series of rectangles used as ornamental decoration in cornices. Example: 187-195 Broadway	

Dichromatic brickwork: the use of two colours of brick, tile or slate to decorate a façade. Example: 299 Broadway	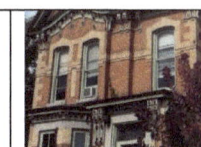
Dormer: (French for "sleep") a gable end window that pierces through the plane of a sloping roof surface to create usable space in the top floor or attic of a building by adding headroom. Example: 135-139 Broadway	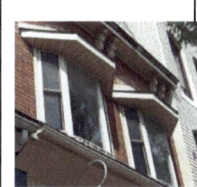
Gable: the triangular portion of a wall between the edges of a sloping roof. Example: 78 Broadway	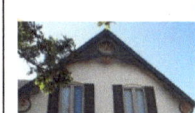
Gambrel Roof: a symmetrical two-sided roof with two slopes on each side; the upper slope is positioned at a shallow angle, while the lower slope is steep. It is similar to a mansard roof, but a gambrel has vertical gable ends instead of being hipped at the four corners of the building. Example: 239 Broadway	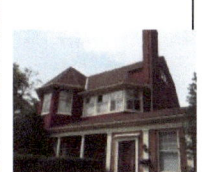
Hipped Roof: a roof where all sides slope downwards to the walls with no gables. Example: Old Fire Hall	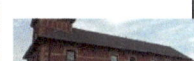
Keystones and Voussoirs: a voussoir is a wedge-shaped element used in building an arch. A keystone is the central stone that locks all the stones into position, allowing the arch to bear weight. A keystone is often enlarged and embellished. Example: 87 Broadway, Orangeville Town Hall	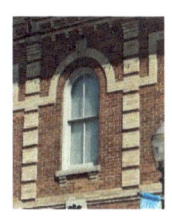

Lancet Window: a tall, narrow window with a pointed arch at its top. Example: 247 Broadway	
Palladian Window: a large window that is divided into three sections with the centre section larger than the two side sections and usually arched. Example: 65 Broadway	
Pediment: a triangular section above the horizontal structure (entablature), typically supported by columns. The inside of the triangle is called the tympanum. Example: 269 Broadway	
Pilaster: a slightly projecting column built into or applied to the face of a wall for additional structural support. Example: 148 Broadway	
Quoin: masonry blocks at the corner of a wall, often a decorative feature, usually larger or of a different colour than the rest of the wall. Example: Orangeville Public Library	

Rose Window: a circular window with ornamental tracery radiating from the centre. Example: 247 Broadway, Westminster United Church	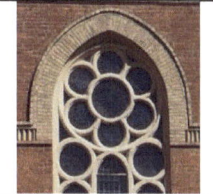
Sidelight: a window, usually with a vertical emphasis, that flanks a door, and is often used to emphasize the importance of a primary entrance. Example: 238 Broadway	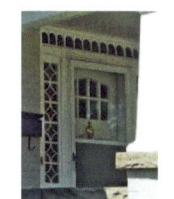
Vergeboards: also called bargeboards – hang from the projecting end of a roof and are often elaborately carved and ornamented. Example: 283 Broadway	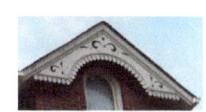
Window Hood: A hood is the piece found above window openings, usually of an ornate design, and covers the top third of the opening. Hoods are commonly placed above arched or curved openings on both windows and doors. Example: 148 Broadway	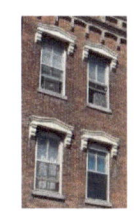

Orangeville's Building Styles

Beaux Arts: Promoters of this style sought to express the classical principles on a grand and imposing scale. Many of the Beaux Arts buildings were banks, post offices, and railway stations. The Ontario Beaux Arts style is eclectic mixing elements of Classical, Renaissance and Baroque. Often the designs have a temple-like façade, pedimented porticos, balustrades, capitals in many styles Example: Orangeville Public Library	
Edwardian, 1900-1930 – This style bridges the ornate and elaborate styles of the Victorian era and the simplified styles of the 20th century. Balanced facades, simple roof lines, dormer windows, large front porches, and smooth brick surfaces are its characteristics. Example: 65 Broadway	
Georgian, before 1860 – This style began with the British King Georges in the 18th century. These buildings have balanced facades around a central door, medium-pitched gable roofs, and small paned windows. Example: 260 Broadway	
Gothic Revival, 1830-1890 – These decorative buildings have sharply-pitched gables with highly detailed vergeboards, pointed-arch window openings, and dichromatic brickwork. It is a common style in Ontario. Examples: 301 Broadway	

Italianate, 1850-1900 – It has wide-bracketed eaves, belvederes, wrap-around verandahs. Example: 236 Broadway	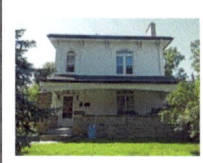
Queen Anne, 1885-1900 – This style is distinguished by an irregular outline featuring a combination of an offset tower, broad gables, projecting two-storey bays, verandahs, multi-sloped roofs, and tall, decorative chimneys. A mixture of brick and wood is common. Windows often have one large single-paned bottom sash and small panes in the upper sash. Example: 239 Broadway	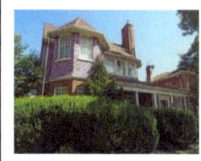
Regency Cottage, 1830-1860 – This style originated in England in 1815 and spread to Ontario later in the 19th century as British officers retired to Canada. It is a modest one-storey house with a low-pitched hip roof and has a symmetrical front façade. Example: 238 Broadway	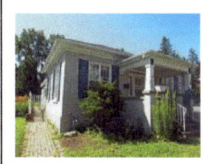
Romanesque Revival, 1880-1910 – This style hearkens back to medieval architecture of the 11th and 12th centuries with a heavy appearance, blocky towers and rounded arches. Example: 283 Broadway	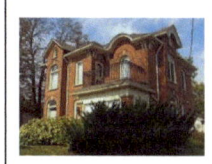

www.ingramcontent.com/pod-product-compliance
Lightning Source LLC
Chambersburg PA
CBHW040923180526
45159CB00002BA/584